Introduction to Ethical Hacking and Penetration Testing

Protect Your Systems by Understanding
Cybersecurity Attacks

THOMPSON CARTER

TABLE OF CONTENTS

Introduction

In today's interconnected world, cybersecurity has never been more critical. Every day, organizations, governments, and individuals are exposed to a growing number of cyber threats—from sophisticated hacking attempts to malicious software and data breaches. The rise in cybercrime and the increasing complexity of attacks have made it evident that traditional security measures are no longer enough. To protect sensitive information, prevent financial loss, and maintain public trust, organizations must take proactive steps to identify and address vulnerabilities before they can be exploited. This is where ethical hacking plays a crucial role.

Ethical hacking, also known as **penetration testing**, is the process of identifying and exploiting vulnerabilities in systems, networks, and applications with the permission of the owner, in order to uncover potential security flaws. Unlike malicious hackers, ethical hackers are trained professionals who work to improve security by discovering weaknesses before they can be used for harmful purposes. By simulating the methods of cybercriminals, ethical hackers help organizations protect their most valuable assets, including sensitive data, intellectual property, and customer information.

The role of an ethical hacker is multifaceted and requires a combination of technical expertise, problem-solving skills, and a deep understanding of cyber threats. Ethical hackers use a wide range of tools and techniques, from scanning for vulnerabilities and exploiting weaknesses to analyzing malware and conducting social engineering attacks. However, this book aims to simplify the process and present it in a structured, easy-to-understand format for those who are new to the field or looking to expand their knowledge.

This book, *Introduction to Ethical Hacking and Penetration Testing*, is designed to provide a comprehensive guide to ethical hacking, covering everything from the basics to advanced techniques. Whether you're a beginner looking to enter the field of cybersecurity or an experienced professional seeking to sharpen your skills, this book will serve as an invaluable resource. Through practical examples, real-world case studies, and actionable advice, you will gain a thorough understanding of how penetration testing works and how to conduct tests ethically and effectively.

Why This Book Is Important

As cyberattacks become more sophisticated, the demand for skilled ethical hackers continues to rise. Organizations across industries are seeking professionals who can identify weaknesses in their systems before they are targeted by malicious actors. Ethical hacking is no longer just an option—it is a necessity in safeguarding sensitive information, maintaining regulatory compliance, and preserving an organization's reputation.

However, ethical hacking is not without its challenges. It requires a deep understanding of technology, security protocols, and hacking techniques. It also demands a strong ethical foundation, as ethical hackers must navigate the fine line between testing systems for vulnerabilities and respecting the privacy of individuals and organizations. This book will provide you with the knowledge, tools, and ethical framework to conduct effective penetration tests while upholding the highest standards of professionalism.

Who This Book Is For

This book is intended for anyone interested in learning about ethical hacking and penetration testing. Whether you are a:

- **Beginner** with no prior experience in cybersecurity, seeking a comprehensive introduction to ethical hacking concepts, tools, and techniques.
- **IT professional** with a basic understanding of networking or system administration, looking to transition into cybersecurity and learn how to apply penetration testing skills.
- **Cybersecurity student** pursuing a career in ethical hacking or penetration testing, eager to expand your knowledge and gain hands-on insights into real-world vulnerabilities.

- **Security practitioner** interested in honing your skills or expanding your expertise in penetration testing and ethical hacking to stay ahead of emerging threats.

You will find valuable insights, practical exercises, and case studies that cover the most relevant topics in the field of ethical hacking.

What You Will Learn

In this book, you will gain a detailed understanding of ethical hacking and penetration testing, learning not only the tools and techniques but also the ethical principles that guide these practices. Each chapter is structured to build upon the previous one, allowing you to progressively develop your knowledge and skills. Key topics include:

- **Understanding Cybersecurity Threats**: Identifying and analyzing the different types of threats, including viruses, worms, ransomware, and social engineering attacks.
- **Penetration Testing Process**: Understanding the phases of penetration testing, from reconnaissance and information gathering to exploitation and reporting.
- **Ethical Hacking Tools**: Introduction to the most commonly used penetration testing tools like Nmap, Wireshark, and Burp Suite, and how to effectively use them.

- **Vulnerability Assessment and Exploitation**: Learning how to scan for vulnerabilities, exploit weaknesses, and understand the ethical and legal considerations involved.
- **Advanced Techniques**: Delving into advanced topics like pivoting, exploitation chaining, and dealing with zero-day vulnerabilities.
- **Specialized Penetration Testing**: Exploring industry-specific testing, such as testing in finance, healthcare, and government sectors, and understanding the unique challenges in these environments.
- **Reporting and Communication**: How to write clear and actionable penetration testing reports, ensuring your findings are easily understood by both technical and non-technical stakeholders.

The Path Ahead

As you journey through the chapters of this book, you will not only gain technical expertise in ethical hacking and penetration testing but also learn how to approach cybersecurity challenges from an ethical and professional standpoint. The goal is not just to teach you how to exploit vulnerabilities, but also to help you understand how to think like a hacker, assess risks, and make informed decisions to protect digital assets and data.

The ultimate aim of this book is to provide you with the knowledge and confidence to become a skilled and ethical cybersecurity professional. By the end of the book, you will have the foundation to embark on a career in ethical hacking, pursue certification, or simply gain a deeper understanding of how to secure systems and networks.

Conclusion

Cybersecurity is one of the most exciting and fast-paced fields in technology today. The skills of an ethical hacker are in high demand, and the opportunities for those who excel in this area are vast. Ethical hackers are essential to the safety and security of organizations around the world, and this book will guide you on your path to becoming one of them.

Through this guide, we hope to inspire you to embrace the challenge of ethical hacking, learn new skills, and make a meaningful impact in the world of cybersecurity. Whether you aim to work in a corporate environment, start your own cybersecurity consultancy, or contribute to global efforts in securing the digital landscape, the journey to becoming an ethical hacker begins here.

Chapter 1: Introduction to Ethical Hacking

What is Ethical Hacking?

Ethical hacking, often referred to as penetration testing or white-hat hacking, is the practice of intentionally probing computer systems, networks, or web applications to uncover security weaknesses that could potentially be exploited by malicious hackers. Unlike cybercriminals, ethical hackers follow a structured methodology and obtain explicit permission from the system's owner before conducting any form of testing or scanning. Their primary objective is to identify and fix vulnerabilities before they can be exploited for harmful purposes. This proactive approach helps organizations strengthen their defenses and avoid potential data breaches, financial losses, or reputational damage.

Ethical hackers use the same tools and techniques as malicious hackers (black-hat hackers) but with permission and in a controlled, legal context. The goal of ethical hacking is not to exploit the vulnerabilities but to expose them and help the organization fortify its cybersecurity infrastructure. By identifying security weaknesses, ethical hackers provide valuable insights that can guide businesses in enhancing their security posture.

An essential aspect of ethical hacking is that it is conducted within ethical boundaries. Ethical hackers are expected to respect the rules and boundaries set forth by the organization commissioning the test. They are also bound by strict codes of conduct and must act in the best interest of the organization and its stakeholders. This is what distinguishes ethical hacking from malicious hacking, where the intention is to cause harm or steal sensitive information.

The Importance of Ethical Hackers in Cybersecurity

The importance of ethical hackers in cybersecurity cannot be overstated, especially in a world where cyberattacks are becoming more sophisticated and frequent. Organizations, regardless of their size or industry, rely on cybersecurity experts to protect their digital assets. Ethical hackers play a pivotal role in preventing these assets from falling victim to malicious hackers.

1. **Identifying Vulnerabilities Before Attackers Do**: The primary role of ethical hackers is to find weaknesses within a system that could be exploited by attackers. This includes vulnerabilities in software, hardware, networks, or configurations that could allow unauthorized access. Ethical hackers test these weaknesses in a controlled environment and provide actionable recommendations to secure them before an attacker can exploit them.

2. **Minimizing Financial and Reputation Losses**: Cyberattacks can cause significant financial damage and reputational harm to an organization. A successful attack can lead to stolen customer data, financial fraud, intellectual property theft, or system outages. Ethical hackers help prevent these outcomes by identifying weaknesses that could potentially lead to such consequences.

3. **Improving System and Network Security**: Ethical hacking tests the effectiveness of existing security measures. By identifying weaknesses and vulnerabilities, ethical hackers can recommend stronger defenses and strategies to improve the overall security of the system. This could involve patching software, configuring firewalls, implementing multi-factor authentication, or enhancing user training to prevent phishing attacks.

4. **Ensuring Compliance with Regulations**: Many industries, such as healthcare, finance, and retail, are subject to stringent regulations that require organizations to safeguard sensitive information. Ethical hackers help organizations adhere to these regulations by conducting penetration tests that ensure their systems are secure and compliant with relevant laws, such as GDPR, HIPAA, and PCI DSS.

5. **Testing Real-World Attacks**: Ethical hackers simulate the tactics, techniques, and procedures (TTPs) used by malicious hackers to see how well a system can defend

against real-world attacks. This includes testing for vulnerabilities such as SQL injection, cross-site scripting (XSS), denial-of-service attacks, and social engineering tactics. By simulating actual cyberattacks, ethical hackers help organizations understand the full scope of potential threats and improve their defenses accordingly.

6. **Enhancing Incident Response Plans**: Ethical hackers not only identify vulnerabilities but also assist organizations in improving their incident response plans. Through penetration testing and simulated attacks, ethical hackers can help organizations understand how quickly they can detect, respond to, and recover from a cyberattack. This improves their ability to minimize damage in the event of a real attack.

Key Differences Between Ethical Hacking and Malicious Hacking

While both ethical hacking and malicious hacking may involve similar techniques and tools, the core differences lie in intent, permission, and legality. Understanding these distinctions is crucial for grasping the ethical boundaries and responsibilities of ethical hackers.

1. **Intent**: The most fundamental difference between ethical hackers and malicious hackers is intent. Ethical hackers are motivated by the desire to protect systems, identify

weaknesses, and improve security. They work in collaboration with organizations to ensure that security measures are strong and reliable. Malicious hackers, on the other hand, are driven by personal gain, revenge, or ideologies. They exploit vulnerabilities to steal data, damage systems, or disrupt services.

2. **Permission**: Ethical hackers always operate with explicit permission from the system owner, ensuring that their activities are legal and authorized. Before performing any penetration testing, ethical hackers sign a contract or agreement that defines the scope of the test, the systems to be tested, and the methods to be used. This permission sets ethical hackers apart from malicious hackers, who engage in hacking activities without any consent, often violating the law in the process.

3. **Objectives**: Ethical hackers aim to uncover vulnerabilities to help organizations patch them before they can be exploited. Their goal is to protect the integrity, confidentiality, and availability of systems and data. Malicious hackers, conversely, often exploit vulnerabilities for financial gain, intellectual property theft, or simply to cause harm. They do not work to enhance security or protect the systems they target.

4. **Legality**: Ethical hacking is legal and carried out within the boundaries of the law, whereas malicious hacking is illegal

and criminal. Ethical hackers follow guidelines and legal frameworks such as the Computer Fraud and Abuse Act (CFAA) and the Digital Millennium Copyright Act (DMCA) to ensure their activities are within legal bounds. Malicious hackers, however, break laws and are subject to prosecution if caught.

5. **Accountability and Responsibility**: Ethical hackers are accountable for their actions, often working under the supervision of a designated authority within an organization. They must report any vulnerabilities they discover and assist in remediating them. Malicious hackers bear no responsibility for the damage they cause and actively attempt to cover their tracks to avoid detection and prosecution.

6. **Public Impact**: Ethical hackers work to prevent security breaches, protect sensitive data, and safeguard users' privacy. Their efforts contribute to the overall stability and security of the digital world. Malicious hackers, however, create chaos by compromising data, attacking critical infrastructure, and causing widespread harm to individuals and organizations.

Legal Considerations and the Role of Certifications

Ethical hacking operates within a legal framework that ensures the protection of privacy, intellectual property, and organizational assets. It is essential for ethical hackers to understand the legal implications of their activities to avoid crossing any ethical or legal boundaries.

1. **Legal Frameworks for Ethical Hacking**: Ethical hackers must operate within the confines of various legal frameworks that define what is permissible in terms of testing and accessing systems. These legal guidelines help ensure that ethical hackers do not overstep their bounds and that they conduct testing in a manner that is lawful and ethical. Ethical hackers are often required to obtain written authorization from organizations before performing penetration tests, ensuring that all activities are conducted with the organization's consent.

2. **Computer Fraud and Abuse Act (CFAA)**: In the United States, the CFAA is one of the primary laws that governs hacking activities. The CFAA makes it illegal to access a computer system without authorization, and ethical hackers must ensure they have explicit permission to perform penetration testing. Violating the CFAA can result in criminal charges, fines, and imprisonment.

3. **Digital Millennium Copyright Act (DMCA)**: The DMCA prohibits unauthorized access to copyrighted material and digital content. Ethical hackers must be cautious when accessing systems that contain copyrighted materials,

ensuring they do not inadvertently violate copyright laws during their testing.

4. **Data Protection and Privacy Laws**: Ethical hackers must adhere to data protection and privacy laws, such as the General Data Protection Regulation (GDPR) in Europe or the Health Insurance Portability and Accountability Act (HIPAA) in the United States. These laws govern how personal data is collected, stored, and processed. Ethical hackers must take care not to violate these laws by exposing sensitive data during penetration testing.

5. **Certifications for Ethical Hackers**: Certifications play a vital role in ensuring that ethical hackers possess the necessary knowledge and skills to perform their duties effectively. Some of the most recognized certifications in the field of ethical hacking include:

   o **Certified Ethical Hacker (CEH)**: The CEH certification, offered by EC-Council, is one of the most widely recognized credentials for ethical hackers. It demonstrates a professional's ability to identify vulnerabilities and implement effective countermeasures.

   o **Offensive Security Certified Professional (OSCP)**: Offered by Offensive Security, the OSCP certification is known for its practical, hands-on approach to penetration testing. OSCP holders must prove their ability to exploit vulnerabilities in real-world environments.

- o **CompTIA Security+**: While not specific to ethical hacking, Security+ is a foundational cybersecurity certification that covers a broad range of topics, including network security, cryptography, and risk management.

Certifications provide ethical hackers with the credibility and knowledge needed to pursue careers in cybersecurity. They also ensure that ethical hackers stay up-to-date with the latest tools, techniques, and best practices in the ever-evolving cybersecurity landscape.

This chapter gives a comprehensive introduction to ethical hacking, its importance, the distinction between ethical and malicious hacking, and the legal frameworks that guide the profession. It sets the foundation for the reader to understand the responsibilities, tools, and methodologies used by ethical hackers. The next chapters will dive deeper into the various tools, techniques, and processes involved in ethical hacking and penetration testing.

Chapter 2: Understanding Cybersecurity Threats

Common Cybersecurity Threats

Cybersecurity threats are constantly evolving as technology advances and new vulnerabilities are discovered. The landscape of cyber threats is diverse, encompassing a variety of malicious activities aimed at breaching systems, stealing data, or causing damage. Understanding these threats is the first step in building an effective defense strategy. This section explores some of the most common types of cybersecurity threats: viruses, worms, ransomware, and other prevalent attacks.

1. Viruses

A virus is a type of malicious software (malware) that attaches itself to a legitimate program or file in order to spread from one computer to another. Once executed, a virus can damage system files, corrupt data, or render systems unusable.

- **How it works**: Viruses require human intervention to propagate. A user must open or execute an infected file for the virus to activate. The virus then replicates itself, often attaching to executable files or documents. It may spread via email attachments, infected websites, or external storage devices (USB drives, for example).

- **Real-world example**: The *ILOVEYOU* virus, which spread via email in 2000, was one of the most destructive viruses in history. It was disguised as a love letter, and once opened, it would email itself to everyone in the victim's contact list, causing widespread damage to both personal and corporate systems.

- **Mitigation**: Antivirus software, regular updates, and education about not opening unknown attachments are essential for preventing virus infections.

2. Worms

Unlike viruses, worms are self-replicating programs that do not require a host program to spread. Worms can propagate across networks without any user interaction, exploiting vulnerabilities in systems to spread from one machine to another.

- **How it works**: Worms generally exploit known vulnerabilities in software or operating systems. Once they find a target, they replicate and spread rapidly, often over networks, email systems, or file-sharing platforms. Worms can cause a denial of service (DoS) by overwhelming systems with traffic or consuming excessive resources.

- **Real-world example**: The *Blaster Worm* (2003) exploited a vulnerability in the Microsoft Windows operating system. It spread rapidly and caused infected systems to crash, leading to a significant disruption in services and downtime for many businesses.

- **Mitigation**: Regular patching and updates to operating systems and software, coupled with proper network security configurations, can help defend against worm attacks.

3. *Ransomware*

Ransomware is a type of malware that encrypts a victim's files or locks them out of their system and demands a ransom (usually in cryptocurrency) to restore access. The threat of permanent data loss or the public release of sensitive data puts immense pressure on victims to comply with the ransom demands.

- **How it works**: Ransomware typically enters a system through phishing emails, malicious websites, or software vulnerabilities. Once executed, it encrypts files, rendering them unreadable without the decryption key. The attacker demands payment for the key to unlock the files.
- **Real-world example**: The *WannaCry* ransomware attack in 2017 affected hundreds of thousands of computers worldwide, causing major disruptions to healthcare, business, and government sectors. It exploited a vulnerability in older versions of Microsoft Windows and demanded payment in Bitcoin to restore access.
- **Mitigation**: The best defense against ransomware is to maintain regular backups of critical data, use strong endpoint

protection, and ensure systems are updated with the latest security patches. Employee awareness training is also essential to avoid falling victim to phishing campaigns that commonly deliver ransomware.

4. Spyware and Adware

Spyware is malicious software designed to secretly gather information from a victim's device without their consent. Adware, a subset of spyware, specifically aims to bombard the user with unsolicited advertisements.

- **How it works**: Spyware typically monitors user activities, such as browsing habits, passwords, and other sensitive information. Adware often tracks browsing habits and displays unwanted advertisements in an intrusive manner, but spyware can be much more insidious, gathering login credentials and financial data.
- **Real-world example**: In 2005, the *Gator* adware (later rebranded as *Claria*) caused controversy by collecting users' browsing data and displaying ads in an invasive way. While not inherently malicious, it often led to privacy violations and was difficult to remove.
- **Mitigation**: Use of reputable antivirus programs, browser extensions, and user vigilance when downloading software from the internet can help prevent spyware and adware infections.

5. *Phishing and Spear Phishing*

Phishing is a type of cyber attack that involves tricking individuals into revealing sensitive information, such as usernames, passwords, or credit card details, typically via fraudulent emails or websites.

- **How it works**: Phishing emails often impersonate legitimate organizations, such as banks or online services, and trick users into clicking malicious links or downloading infected attachments. Spear phishing, a more targeted form of phishing, uses personalized information to make the attack more convincing.

- **Real-world example**: In 2016, the *DNC email leak* occurred when hackers used spear phishing techniques to infiltrate the Democratic National Committee's email system. They used fake email addresses designed to look like legitimate communication from trusted sources to trick individuals into divulging login credentials.

- **Mitigation**: Educating users on how to recognize phishing attempts, implementing multi-factor authentication (MFA), and using anti-phishing tools can help reduce the likelihood of falling victim to these attacks.

Threat Actors: Hackers, Insiders, Cybercriminals

Understanding the types of individuals or groups responsible for cybersecurity threats is crucial in developing effective defense strategies. Cyberattacks are not just carried out by individuals with technical skills; various threat actors with different motives exist, each posing unique risks.

1. Hackers

Hackers are individuals who use their technical expertise to manipulate or compromise systems. While hackers are often associated with malicious activities, not all hackers are bad. Hackers can be classified into different categories based on their intent and actions:

- **Black-hat hackers**: These are malicious hackers who exploit vulnerabilities for personal gain or to cause harm. They often engage in illegal activities such as stealing data, spreading malware, or defacing websites.
- **White-hat hackers**: Ethical hackers or penetration testers who use their skills to find vulnerabilities in systems to help organizations secure them. They work with permission and within legal boundaries to improve cybersecurity.
- **Grey-hat hackers**: These hackers fall somewhere between black-hat and white-hat hackers. They may uncover vulnerabilities without permission but report them to the affected organization without exploiting them. However, their actions can still be illegal.

2. Insiders

Insiders are individuals within an organization who have authorized access to its systems or data but misuse that access to cause harm. Insiders may be employees, contractors, or business partners who have intimate knowledge of the organization's operations.

- **Malicious insiders**: Employees or contractors who intentionally misuse their access to steal data or disrupt operations. Often motivated by personal gain, revenge, or financial incentives, malicious insiders can cause significant damage.
- **Negligent insiders**: These individuals do not intentionally cause harm but make mistakes that expose the organization to threats, such as falling for phishing attacks, misconfiguring security settings, or mishandling sensitive data.

3. Cybercriminals

Cybercriminals are individuals or organized groups who engage in illegal online activities to profit from their actions. Cybercriminals may target individuals, corporations, or government entities for various reasons, including financial gain, political motives, or personal vendettas.

- **Hacktivists**: These are individuals or groups who hack systems for political or ideological reasons. They often target organizations or governments that they believe are engaged in unethical practices. Famous examples include the *Anonymous* group, which has carried out numerous politically motivated cyberattacks.

- **State-sponsored hackers**: Some cybercriminals are employed by governments or nation-states to conduct cyber espionage, sabotage, or warfare. These attackers typically target critical infrastructure, corporate secrets, or intelligence data.

The Anatomy of a Cyber Attack

To fully understand how cybersecurity threats manifest, it is essential to grasp the anatomy of a typical cyber attack. A cyber attack generally follows a sequence of stages, each involving specific tactics, techniques, and procedures (TTPs) used by attackers.

1. Reconnaissance

The first stage of a cyber attack is gathering information about the target. Attackers perform reconnaissance to identify potential weaknesses and gather as much information as possible about the target's systems, personnel, and vulnerabilities.

- **Passive reconnaissance**: This involves collecting publicly available information, such as from websites, social media, or public databases, without directly interacting with the target's systems.

- **Active reconnaissance**: In this phase, attackers actively interact with the target's systems, such as scanning networks or testing for open ports.

2. Weaponization

Once the attacker has gathered sufficient information, they prepare a weapon to exploit a vulnerability. This could involve crafting malware, phishing emails, or other malicious code designed to exploit a specific weakness identified in the reconnaissance phase.

3. Delivery

In this phase, the attacker delivers the weaponized attack to the target. This could be done via email attachments, malicious links, infected USB drives, or through exploiting a vulnerability in a website or web application.

4. Exploitation

Once the attack has been delivered, the malicious code is executed, exploiting the identified vulnerability. This could involve installing malware, triggering a buffer overflow, or gaining unauthorized access to the system.

5. Installation

The attacker then installs a backdoor, remote access tool, or other persistent mechanisms to maintain control over the compromised system. This allows them to continue their attack or to use the system as a springboard for further exploitation.

6. Command and Control (C2)

After gaining access, the attacker establishes a communication channel (C2) with the compromised system, allowing them to send commands, control the system remotely, or exfiltrate data without detection.

7. Exfiltration

At this stage, the attacker begins to exfiltrate valuable data from the target. This could include sensitive personal information, financial data, intellectual property, or access credentials.

8. Action on Objectives

In the final stage, the attacker achieves their primary goal, which could be stealing data, disrupting services, damaging the target's reputation, or causing financial loss. In some cases, the attacker may also attempt to cover their tracks to avoid detection.

By understanding the common cybersecurity threats, threat actors, and the anatomy of a cyber attack, individuals and organizations can better defend themselves against potential breaches. The next chapter will explore the tools and methodologies used by ethical hackers to detect and neutralize these threats.

Chapter 3: The Ethical Hacker's Toolkit

Overview of Tools Used in Ethical Hacking

An ethical hacker's toolkit is essential for conducting thorough penetration testing, vulnerability assessments, and security audits. Ethical hackers utilize a wide range of tools to assess the security of computer systems, networks, and web applications. These tools are designed to automate tasks, identify vulnerabilities, and exploit weaknesses in a controlled, ethical manner to help organizations improve their security posture. The tools used in ethical hacking vary based on the scope of the test, the target system, and the specific vulnerabilities being assessed. The overall objective of using these tools is not to cause harm but to discover vulnerabilities before they can be exploited by malicious hackers.

An effective toolkit for ethical hacking includes software tools for reconnaissance, scanning, exploitation, post-exploitation, reporting, and securing the system. Each category of tools serves a different purpose and is utilized at various stages of the penetration testing process. Ethical hackers typically use a combination of commercial and open-source tools, ensuring a comprehensive and cost-effective approach to penetration testing.

Ethical hackers must be familiar with a wide range of tools, as they may need to address different types of vulnerabilities across diverse systems. The selection of tools depends on the target environment (web applications, networks, IoT devices, etc.), the type of attack (network infiltration, social engineering, password cracking), and the complexity of the system.

Introduction to Popular Tools

While ethical hackers have access to numerous tools, some stand out for their wide use, reliability, and effectiveness in performing a variety of penetration testing tasks. Below are some of the most commonly used tools in ethical hacking:

1. Nmap (Network Mapper)

Nmap is one of the most powerful and widely used network scanning tools in the ethical hacker's arsenal. It is primarily used for network discovery and security auditing. Nmap allows ethical hackers to scan large networks and discover hosts, services, and open ports on the target system.

- **Key Features**:
    - Network discovery and mapping: Nmap can detect live hosts and identify open ports and services running on each host.
    - Operating system detection: Nmap can identify the operating system of the target system based on network traffic patterns.

o Service version detection: It can also detect the version of services running on open ports (e.g., web servers, FTP servers).

o Scripting engine: Nmap has a powerful scripting engine (NSE) that allows hackers to automate specific tasks such as vulnerability scanning, brute-force attacks, and more.

- **How It Works**: Ethical hackers use Nmap to perform a range of tasks, including identifying active devices on a network, mapping the network topology, and discovering open ports. This information is valuable for planning further attack steps or identifying vulnerable services that could be exploited.

- **Real-World Application**: Nmap is often used to scan large networks for weak points. For instance, it can be used to identify servers running outdated services that need to be patched or secured.

2. Wireshark

Wireshark is a popular network protocol analyzer (packet sniffer) that captures and inspects network traffic in real-time. It is an indispensable tool for ethical hackers who need to analyze communication between systems, identify malicious traffic, and understand how data flows within a network.

- **Key Features**:

- o Protocol analysis: Wireshark supports hundreds of network protocols, from basic TCP/IP to advanced protocols like HTTP, FTP, DNS, and more.
- o Real-time packet capture: It captures and displays data packets transmitted over a network in real time, allowing hackers to analyze them for signs of malicious activity.
- o Deep inspection: Wireshark allows hackers to examine the contents of each packet, including headers, payload, and metadata, which can be useful for identifying unauthorized data transfer or vulnerabilities.
- o Filtering capabilities: Wireshark provides powerful filtering options to focus on specific traffic, such as specific IP addresses, ports, or protocol types.

- **How It Works**: Ethical hackers use Wireshark to capture packets on a network and analyze the data to uncover vulnerabilities. For example, Wireshark can be used to detect unencrypted communication, weak authentication mechanisms, or suspicious network activity that could indicate an attack.

- **Real-World Application**: During a penetration test, Wireshark can be used to sniff network traffic to check for unencrypted passwords, sensitive data leaks, or communication with a command-and-control server during a botnet attack.

3. Burp Suite

Burp Suite is one of the most comprehensive and widely used tools for web application penetration testing. It is an integrated platform that allows ethical hackers to identify vulnerabilities in web applications, such as SQL injection, cross-site scripting (XSS), and other common web application attacks.

- **Key Features**:
    - o Intercepting proxy: Burp Suite acts as an intercepting proxy that allows hackers to monitor and modify HTTP(S) traffic between the browser and the server.
    - o Web vulnerability scanning: Burp Suite includes a web vulnerability scanner that automates the process of discovering common vulnerabilities in web applications.
    - o Intruder: Burp Suite's Intruder feature allows hackers to automate brute-force attacks, such as password cracking and cookie manipulation.
    - o Repeater: The Repeater feature is used for manual testing and allows hackers to send requests repeatedly with different payloads to test for vulnerabilities.

- ○ Extensibility: Burp Suite supports a wide range of plugins and extensions that add functionality, such as additional scanning capabilities or integration with other tools.
- **How It Works**: Ethical hackers use Burp Suite to intercept traffic, manipulate requests and responses, and conduct automated scans to identify vulnerabilities. Burp Suite's vulnerability scanner automates the process of identifying issues like SQL injection, cross-site scripting, and other vulnerabilities in web applications.
- **Real-World Application**: Burp Suite is widely used in web application penetration testing to check for common web-based vulnerabilities. For instance, ethical hackers can use Burp Suite to test an e-commerce site for potential injection vulnerabilities that could allow attackers to gain access to sensitive customer data.

4. Metasploit Framework

Metasploit is a well-known penetration testing framework used for developing and executing exploit code against remote target machines. It is particularly useful for testing network security, exploiting vulnerabilities, and gaining access to target systems.

- **Key Features**:

- o Exploit development: Metasploit provides a range of pre-built exploits and payloads that ethical hackers can use to test for vulnerabilities in systems.
- o Post-exploitation: Once a system is compromised, Metasploit helps ethical hackers gather information, escalate privileges, and maintain access to the target.
- o Meterpreter: Meterpreter is a powerful Metasploit payload that allows ethical hackers to execute commands on a compromised system remotely, collect data, and maintain control over the system.
- o Integration with other tools: Metasploit integrates well with other penetration testing tools, including Nmap, for a seamless testing experience.
- **How It Works**: Ethical hackers use Metasploit to exploit vulnerabilities discovered during reconnaissance and scanning phases. After exploiting a vulnerability, Metasploit can be used to gain access to a target system and execute post-exploitation tasks, such as exfiltrating data or installing a backdoor.
- **Real-World Application**: Metasploit is often used to exploit unpatched vulnerabilities in operating systems and applications. For example, ethical hackers can use Metasploit to exploit an unpatched flaw in a web server and gain access to sensitive files.

5. John the Ripper

John the Ripper (often abbreviated to "John") is a popular password cracking tool used to identify weak passwords by performing dictionary and brute-force attacks.

- **Key Features**:
  - Cracking password hashes: John the Ripper can crack password hashes in a variety of formats, including those used by UNIX, Windows, and other operating systems.
  - Wordlist-based cracking: John uses wordlists to attempt to crack passwords. It can also perform sophisticated attacks like rule-based cracking to increase success rates.
  - GPU support: John the Ripper can leverage Graphics Processing Units (GPUs) to significantly speed up the cracking process, making it a powerful tool for testing password strength.
- **How It Works**: Ethical hackers use John the Ripper to perform password cracking exercises on password hashes, attempting to recover plaintext passwords. It is often used in conjunction with other tools to test the strength of passwords within an organization's network.
- **Real-World Application**: John the Ripper is frequently used to test the strength of hashed passwords stored in

databases. For example, an ethical hacker might use John to check the password complexity of an organization's employees to identify weak passwords that could be exploited in a real-world attack.

The Importance of Maintaining a Toolkit for Penetration Testing

Maintaining an up-to-date and effective toolkit is critical for ethical hackers who wish to conduct thorough penetration tests and security assessments. A well-maintained toolkit enables ethical hackers to efficiently identify vulnerabilities, exploit weaknesses, and provide actionable recommendations to improve security. Here are several reasons why maintaining a toolkit is essential:

1. **Comprehensive Testing**: A diverse set of tools allows ethical hackers to test all aspects of a system's security, including network, application, and endpoint security. Different tools excel at different tasks, and having the right tools for the job ensures comprehensive coverage of potential vulnerabilities.

2. **Efficiency and Speed**: Ethical hackers use automated tools to speed up tasks such as network scanning, vulnerability detection, and password cracking. This efficiency allows

them to focus on higher-level analysis and remediation rather than spending time on repetitive tasks.

3. **Adaptability**: The cybersecurity landscape is constantly evolving, with new vulnerabilities and attack techniques emerging regularly. By maintaining a current toolkit, ethical hackers can stay ahead of these changes and respond to new threats effectively.

4. **Legal and Ethical Compliance**: Ethical hacking must be performed within legal boundaries and ethical guidelines. Using trusted, reputable tools ensures that ethical hackers can conduct their tests in a manner that complies with industry standards and legal requirements.

5. **Reporting and Documentation**: Many tools in the ethical hacker's toolkit also offer features for generating reports and documenting findings. These reports are crucial for communicating vulnerabilities, attack scenarios, and mitigation strategies to clients or stakeholders.

In summary, the ethical hacker's toolkit consists of a wide variety of tools that serve different purposes throughout the penetration testing process. From network scanning with Nmap to web application testing with Burp Suite and exploiting vulnerabilities with Metasploit, each tool plays a crucial role in identifying and mitigating security threats. By maintaining an up-to-date toolkit, ethical hackers can efficiently test systems, uncover weaknesses, and help organizations improve their overall cybersecurity defenses.

Chapter 4: The Penetration Testing Process

Phases of Penetration Testing: Planning, Discovery, Attack, and Reporting

Penetration testing is a systematic process designed to identify vulnerabilities in computer systems, networks, or web applications and exploit them to assess the potential damage a real-world attacker could cause. Ethical hackers follow a structured process, ensuring that each stage is thoroughly executed and the testing is both effective and compliant with legal and organizational standards.

The penetration testing process is typically broken down into four distinct phases: **Planning**, **Discovery**, **Attack**, and **Reporting**. Each phase serves a unique purpose and builds upon the previous one to ensure that the testing is comprehensive, organized, and delivers actionable results. Let's explore each phase in more detail.

1. Planning Phase

The planning phase, also known as the **pre-engagement phase**, is the most crucial part of any penetration test. During this phase, the scope, objectives, and rules of engagement are established. A well-planned penetration test ensures that the testing process is structured and avoids legal issues, ethical dilemmas, and unintentional disruptions.

- **Key Activities**:
  - **Define the Scope**: The scope outlines which systems, applications, and networks will be tested and which ones will be excluded. This prevents unauthorized testing and ensures that both the ethical hacker and the client understand the boundaries.
  - **Set Objectives**: Objectives must be clearly defined. Are you testing the resilience of a network against denial-of-service (DoS) attacks, assessing the security of web applications, or attempting to gain access to sensitive data? The goals must be aligned with the client's needs.
  - **Obtain Authorization**: Authorization to perform the penetration test is critical. Ethical hackers need explicit written consent from the organization to avoid potential legal consequences.
  - **Establish Rules of Engagement**: This outlines the rules under which the test will be conducted, including the timing of tests, communication channels, and emergency procedures in case critical systems are affected during the test.
  - **Risk Management**: Ethical hackers assess the risks involved in testing, including the possibility of system downtime or service disruption. Precautions are taken to mitigate these risks.

- **Real-World Example**: A financial institution may request a penetration test to identify potential vulnerabilities in their online banking platform. The planning phase will involve defining which specific parts of the platform (e.g., login, payment processing) will be tested, identifying sensitive areas such as customer account data, and determining if social engineering tactics should be part of the test.

2. Discovery Phase

The discovery phase, also known as **reconnaissance** or **information gathering**, is where ethical hackers collect as much information as possible about the target system. The goal is to understand the structure of the system, identify potential attack vectors, and gather critical data that can help inform the next steps in the penetration test.

- **Key Activities**:
  - **Passive Reconnaissance**: Ethical hackers perform passive reconnaissance to gather publicly available information without directly interacting with the target. This can include domain names, IP addresses, network architecture, or employee data from publicly available sources like social media or WHOIS databases.
  - **Active Reconnaissance**: This involves actively probing the target's network and systems to gather

more specific information, such as open ports, services, and operating systems in use. Techniques like network scanning and vulnerability scanning are often employed during this stage.

  o **Fingerprinting**: Identifying and cataloging information about the target's network, systems, or applications, including identifying versions of software, operating systems, or hardware that may have known vulnerabilities.

- **Tools and Techniques**:

  o **Nmap**: Used for network mapping and scanning open ports and services. Nmap is an essential tool during discovery to map out a network and identify live hosts and services.

  o **Shodan**: A search engine that allows ethical hackers to search for internet-connected devices and gather publicly available data about their configurations.

  o **Google Dorking**: Using advanced Google search techniques to gather information about a target's exposed files, directories, or server vulnerabilities.

  o **Recon-ng**: An open-source reconnaissance tool that allows ethical hackers to automate data collection from multiple sources.

- **Real-World Example**: During the discovery phase, a penetration tester hired to test the security of a healthcare organization's network might search publicly available data about the organization's employees, uncover information about the types of devices used by employees, or even find login pages and web servers exposed to the public.

3. Attack Phase

The attack phase, also known as **exploitation**, is where ethical hackers actively attempt to exploit vulnerabilities discovered during the discovery phase. The goal of the attack phase is to simulate what a real-world attacker might do once they've identified vulnerabilities in a system. This phase can involve various techniques, including exploiting misconfigurations, weak passwords, or software vulnerabilities to gain unauthorized access.

- **Key Activities**:
    - **Exploiting Vulnerabilities**: Ethical hackers use known exploits or create custom exploits to gain access to systems. This may involve exploiting unpatched software, misconfigured services, or weak authentication mechanisms.
    - **Privilege Escalation**: Once access is gained, ethical hackers attempt to escalate privileges to gain greater control over the system, mimicking what a malicious attacker would do to move laterally within the environment.

- o **Social Engineering**: In some cases, social engineering tactics (phishing, pretexting, baiting) may be employed to trick users into disclosing credentials or other sensitive information.

- o **Bypassing Security Measures**: Ethical hackers may attempt to bypass security mechanisms, such as firewalls, intrusion detection systems (IDS), or multi-factor authentication, to penetrate deeper into the system.

- **Tools and Techniques**:
  - o **Metasploit**: A framework for exploiting known vulnerabilities and developing custom exploits. Metasploit can be used to test a wide range of exploits and automate attacks.

  - o **Burp Suite**: A tool for exploiting vulnerabilities in web applications, such as SQL injection, cross-site scripting (XSS), and file inclusion vulnerabilities.

  - o **Hydra**: A password-cracking tool that can be used to brute-force login credentials for various protocols, including SSH, FTP, HTTP, and others.

  - o **Aircrack-ng**: A tool used for cracking WEP and WPA-PSK keys in wireless networks, allowing ethical hackers to test the security of wireless systems.

- **Real-World Example**: In a corporate penetration test, after discovering that a web application is vulnerable to SQL injection, the ethical hacker might use Burp Suite to inject SQL commands into the login form, gaining unauthorized access to the application's backend and sensitive customer data.

4. Reporting Phase

The reporting phase is where the results of the penetration test are documented and communicated to the client. A penetration test report is a critical deliverable that provides details of the vulnerabilities discovered, how they were exploited, and recommendations for remediation.

- **Key Activities**:
  - **Documenting Findings**: Ethical hackers document every vulnerability discovered, including the technical details of how the vulnerabilities were exploited and the potential impact on the system or organization.
  - **Risk Assessment**: Ethical hackers assess the risks associated with each vulnerability, considering factors such as the potential damage, likelihood of exploitation, and the business impact of an attack.
  - **Providing Remediation Recommendations**: The final report includes specific, actionable

recommendations for mitigating the identified vulnerabilities, such as patching software, changing configurations, implementing access controls, or improving user awareness training.

- o **Executive Summary**: A non-technical executive summary is often included in the report, summarizing the findings and providing high-level recommendations for the management team.

- **Tools and Techniques**:
  - o **Dradis**: An open-source reporting framework that helps ethical hackers organize and document their findings, making it easier to generate a comprehensive report.
  - o **Faraday**: A collaborative penetration testing tool that enables the team to document and track vulnerabilities, facilitating efficient reporting.
  - o **OWASP ZAP**: While primarily a tool for vulnerability scanning, ZAP also allows for creating detailed reports on the security issues found within web applications.

- **Real-World Example**: After testing the internal network of a large corporation, the penetration tester might generate a report detailing vulnerabilities in the organization's file servers, the ability to exploit weak password policies, and SQL injection issues in web applications. Recommendations may include implementing stronger encryption, upgrading software, and enhancing employee training to recognize phishing attacks.

The penetration testing process is a structured and methodical approach to uncovering security weaknesses and vulnerabilities. By following the four phases—**Planning**, **Discovery**, **Attack**, and **Reporting**—ethical hackers can assess an organization's security posture and provide actionable recommendations for strengthening defenses. Each phase involves specific tools and techniques that are used to simulate real-world attacks, assess risks, and document findings in a clear and comprehensive manner. The ultimate goal is to help organizations understand their security vulnerabilities and take the necessary steps to protect their systems, data, and infrastructure from potential cyber threats.

Chapter 5: Reconnaissance and Information Gathering

The Importance of Reconnaissance in Ethical Hacking

Reconnaissance, often referred to as **recon**, is one of the most crucial phases in the ethical hacking process. It involves gathering as much information as possible about the target system or network before actively exploiting vulnerabilities. The goal of reconnaissance is to gather useful data that will help ethical hackers identify attack vectors, plan subsequent stages of penetration testing, and enhance the chances of successfully identifying and exploiting weaknesses in the target's security posture.

In ethical hacking, reconnaissance is typically performed early in the engagement process. This phase is key for both **passive** and **active** information collection and lays the foundation for the attack phase. By identifying weak points, understanding the system architecture, and gathering details about the target, ethical hackers can save time, reduce risks, and better tailor their approach to testing the system's defenses.

There are two main types of reconnaissance:

1. **Passive Reconnaissance**: This approach involves gathering publicly available information without directly interacting

with the target system. The key advantage of passive reconnaissance is that it minimizes the chances of detection by the target.

2. **Active Reconnaissance**: In contrast, active reconnaissance involves direct interaction with the target system or network, such as scanning open ports or performing vulnerability assessments. Although it provides more detailed information, active reconnaissance carries a higher risk of detection by intrusion detection systems (IDS) or firewalls.

Effective reconnaissance enables ethical hackers to build a detailed picture of the target system and identify the best ways to proceed with their testing. By using various techniques and tools during the reconnaissance phase, ethical hackers can increase their chances of finding exploitable vulnerabilities in the next stages of the penetration test.

Techniques for Information Gathering

There are several key techniques that ethical hackers use during reconnaissance to gather relevant information. These techniques fall into broad categories such as **Open Source Intelligence (OSINT)**, **social engineering**, and **footprinting**.

1. Open Source Intelligence (OSINT)

OSINT is the process of collecting information from publicly available sources, including websites, social media, news articles, forums, and government databases. OSINT can provide detailed insights into a target's infrastructure, employees, technology stack, and potential vulnerabilities—all without directly interacting with the target system.

- **Types of OSINT Data:**
    - o **Domain Information**: Information about the target's domain, including its registration details, email addresses, and domain history. Publicly accessible services like WHOIS can reveal who owns a domain and provide other key details.
    - o **Social Media**: Social media platforms (LinkedIn, Twitter, Facebook, etc.) can provide insight into the organization's personnel, organizational structure, and possible attack vectors, such as weak passwords or internal communications.
    - o **Public Databases**: Government, corporate, and educational websites often release public records, such as business registrations, patents, or annual reports, that may contain valuable information.
    - o **Forums and Blogs**: Cybersecurity forums, industry-specific blogs, and online communities may reveal vulnerabilities or configurations that are not widely known but are crucial to understanding the target's infrastructure.

- **Tools and Techniques for OSINT**:
  - **Google Dorking**: By using advanced Google search queries, ethical hackers can uncover information that might be difficult to find otherwise. For example, searching for "site:example.com filetype:pdf", may reveal sensitive documents hosted on the organization's website.
  - **WHOIS Lookup**: WHOIS is a database of domain registration details. By running a WHOIS search on a domain name, ethical hackers can gather information about the owner of a website, including their contact information, location, and the registrar.
  - **Shodan**: Shodan is a search engine that indexes internet-connected devices. It can reveal information about exposed systems, such as routers, servers, and cameras, by scanning IP addresses and reporting publicly accessible devices.
  - **Maltego**: This is a powerful tool for OSINT gathering that allows ethical hackers to visually map relationships between people, organizations, websites, and domains.
- **Real-World Example**: Suppose an ethical hacker is tasked with testing the security of a financial institution. They may begin by performing OSINT gathering, discovering that the organization uses a specific version of an online payment

service. This information can be used to probe for potential vulnerabilities in that service. Additionally, OSINT might reveal the email addresses of key employees, which could be targeted in phishing attacks.

2. Social Engineering

Social engineering is a technique used to manipulate individuals into divulging sensitive information or performing actions that compromise security. While social engineering is typically associated with malicious hacking, ethical hackers may use it as part of a penetration test (with the organization's consent) to simulate realistic attack scenarios.

- **Types of Social Engineering Attacks**:
    o **Phishing**: The attacker impersonates a trusted entity (e.g., a colleague, bank, or service provider) to lure the target into revealing sensitive information, such as login credentials or credit card details.
    o **Pretexting**: This involves creating a fabricated scenario (or pretext) to obtain information. For example, the hacker might pretend to be from the IT department and ask the target for their password for "system maintenance."
    o **Baiting**: This tactic involves offering something desirable, such as free software, music, or a gift, to

entice the target into clicking on a malicious link or downloading an infected file.

- **Tailgating**: The attacker gains unauthorized physical access to a secure building or area by following an authorized person through security doors.

- **Tools and Techniques for Social Engineering**:
  - **Phishing Campaigns**: Ethical hackers may create fake email campaigns to assess how employees interact with unsolicited emails. This allows organizations to identify vulnerable personnel and improve awareness and training.

  - **Pretexting Scripts**: Penetration testers may develop scripts to simulate phone calls or emails requesting sensitive information, helping organizations assess how susceptible employees are to social engineering attacks.

  - **Fake Login Pages**: Ethical hackers may create fake login pages that resemble legitimate websites (e.g., email login) to see if employees unwittingly enter their credentials.

- **Real-World Example**: In a real-world example, ethical hackers might conduct a phishing attack against an organization's employees, using a legitimate-looking email to request their login credentials. If employees fall for the scam and provide their information, it shows a vulnerability in the organization's training and email security protocols.

3. Footprinting

Footprinting involves gathering detailed information about a target's infrastructure, systems, and security measures to create a map of the target's attack surface. This can include details such as IP addresses, domain names, network topologies, and more. Footprinting is a key technique in both passive and active reconnaissance.

- **Key Activities in Footprinting**:
    - o **Identifying IP Addresses**: Ethical hackers use footprinting to discover the range of IP addresses that belong to the target organization, which can then be used for further scanning and vulnerability assessment.
    - o **DNS Interrogation**: By querying the Domain Name System (DNS), ethical hackers can uncover information such as mail servers, name servers, and subdomains that might reveal potential weaknesses.
    - o **Network Mapping**: Footprinting can help ethical hackers map the organization's internal network, including discovering firewalls, routers, and access control points that could be vulnerable to exploitation.

- **Service Identification**: Ethical hackers may perform service identification on open ports or analyze banner information to identify specific versions of services, which can then be targeted for known vulnerabilities.

- **Tools and Techniques for Footprinting**:
  - **Nslookup/Dig**: These command-line tools allow ethical hackers to query DNS records, such as MX records for mail servers, A records for IP addresses, and CNAME records for subdomains.
  - **Nmap**: Nmap, a network scanning tool, can be used to perform footprinting by mapping out live hosts, open ports, and services on a network.
  - **Traceroute**: Traceroute helps ethical hackers trace the path that network packets take from one system to another, revealing information about intermediate routers and network topology.
  - **Netcraft**: Netcraft is a tool that allows hackers to identify the hosting service and technologies used by a target website. This can be valuable for discovering specific vulnerabilities related to the web hosting environment.

- **Real-World Example**: In a penetration test, an ethical hacker may begin footprinting by performing DNS queries to discover subdomains of a target's website. This could lead to the identification of additional web servers, potentially revealing a vulnerable server running outdated software that could be exploited.

Real-World Examples of Effective Reconnaissance

Effective reconnaissance in real-world scenarios often leads to successful penetration testing engagements. Here are some examples of how reconnaissance is put into practice:

1. **Financial Institution Penetration Test**: During a penetration test for a financial institution, the ethical hacker used OSINT techniques to gather information about the organization's management team, discovering several publicly available personal profiles of key executives. These profiles included email addresses, job titles, and even details about their mobile phones and pets, which were later used in a successful phishing attack. The penetration tester also used domain analysis to discover weak subdomains that led to an exposed server running outdated software. By uncovering these vulnerabilities early, the ethical hacker was able to demonstrate how an attacker could bypass the organization's defenses.

2. **Tech Company Penetration Test**: In another case, an ethical hacker performed footprinting and found a series of exposed subdomains and a public-facing API that had poor authentication measures. The reconnaissance phase revealed that the API was connected to sensitive backend systems. The hacker used social engineering techniques to convince an employee to click on a fake security update link, allowing access to internal systems and exposing data that was previously thought to be secure.

Reconnaissance and information gathering are foundational elements of ethical hacking and penetration testing. Through techniques such as OSINT, social engineering, and footprinting, ethical hackers can gather critical information that helps them understand the target system's architecture and security weaknesses. By conducting thorough reconnaissance, ethical hackers can plan their attacks more effectively, improving the chances of uncovering vulnerabilities and helping organizations bolster their defenses before a real-world cybercriminal can exploit them.

Chapter 6: Scanning and Enumeration

Introduction to Network Scanning and Enumeration

Network scanning and enumeration are critical steps in the penetration testing process that follow the reconnaissance phase. These processes are designed to identify the active systems within a network, the services they run, and potential vulnerabilities that could be exploited. While reconnaissance gathers information about a target, scanning and enumeration focus on actively probing and mapping the network to uncover detailed insights that can guide the testing process.

Network scanning involves scanning a network to identify live systems, open ports, and services that may be running on those systems. Scanning helps ethical hackers build a map of the network, which is essential for understanding the potential points of entry for an attack. It allows testers to identify what is accessible, what is hidden, and what might be vulnerable to an exploit.

Enumeration, on the other hand, is the process of gathering specific information about the identified systems and services, such as usernames, shared resources, and more detailed configurations. Enumeration goes beyond basic scanning by actively querying the target systems to gather detailed, actionable information.

Both scanning and enumeration are necessary for identifying potential attack vectors. By performing these actions, ethical hackers can gain deep insights into how a system or network is configured and whether there are weaknesses that malicious hackers could exploit.

Tools and Methods for Scanning Networks

Network scanning is a foundational activity for ethical hackers, and there are several tools and methods available to accomplish this task effectively. These tools provide comprehensive details about the systems on a network, including what services are running, the versions of those services, and whether those services are vulnerable to exploitation.

1. Nmap (Network Mapper)

Nmap is one of the most widely used and versatile network scanning tools in the ethical hacking community. It allows testers to perform several types of scans, from simple port scans to more detailed service discovery and vulnerability scanning.

- **Key Features**:
    - o **Host Discovery**: Nmap can identify live hosts on a network by pinging the target IP range or using techniques like ARP scanning.
    - o **Port Scanning**: Nmap can scan open ports on a system to see which services are listening. This is

important because attackers often exploit open ports to gain unauthorized access.

- o **Service and Version Detection**: By examining the banners returned by services on open ports, Nmap can help identify the version of a service, which is useful for identifying vulnerabilities associated with specific versions.

- o **Operating System Detection**: Nmap can often detect the operating system running on a target system by analyzing the response patterns from open ports.

- o **Vulnerability Scanning**: Nmap's scripting engine (NSE) enables the automation of vulnerability detection using predefined scripts.

- **How It Works**:
  - o Ethical hackers use Nmap to conduct a **TCP scan** of a target's network to determine which ports are open.

  - o Nmap can also perform a **Service Detection Scan** to check for services running on open ports and identify their versions. This helps ethical hackers map out the attack surface.

  - o For a more detailed assessment, Nmap's **OS Detection Scan** can help detect the underlying operating system of a system, which provides further information for subsequent exploitation.

- **Real-World Application**: In a corporate penetration test, Nmap can be used to identify vulnerable web servers running outdated versions of Apache or unpatched versions of FTP servers that could be targeted for exploitation.

2. Netcat (nc)

Netcat is another versatile tool used by ethical hackers for network scanning and penetration testing. Known as the "Swiss army knife" of networking, Netcat can be used for scanning ports, setting up reverse shells, or connecting to remote systems to test services.

- **Key Features**:
  - **Port Scanning**: Netcat can perform simple port scanning to identify which ports are open and listening on a target machine.
  - **Banner Grabbing**: Netcat can be used for banner grabbing to identify service versions and obtain useful information about running services.
  - **Reverse Shells**: Netcat can create reverse shells by connecting to a remote server, enabling attackers (or ethical hackers) to maintain persistent access to a compromised system.
- **How It Works**:
  - Ethical hackers use Netcat to test which ports are open on a target machine and capture service banners

to determine the types and versions of services running.

o Netcat can also be used for more advanced tasks like creating reverse shells to maintain access to a compromised machine during a penetration test.

- **Real-World Application**: In a network pentest, ethical hackers may use Netcat to confirm that a specific service is running on an open port and then attempt to identify vulnerabilities associated with that service.

3. Angry IP Scanner

Angry IP Scanner is an open-source, lightweight network scanner used for scanning IP addresses and ports. While not as feature-rich as Nmap, it is quick and easy to use for basic network scanning tasks.

- **Key Features**:
    - o **IP Range Scanning**: Angry IP Scanner allows testers to scan a range of IP addresses to see which ones are active.
    - o **Port Scanning**: It can quickly scan ports for open services on a target network.
    - o **Fast and Simple**: Angry IP Scanner is known for its speed and ease of use, making it a great tool for quickly discovering live hosts and services.
- **How It Works**:

- o Ethical hackers use Angry IP Scanner to quickly scan a local network or a specific IP range to identify which systems are up and which ports are open.
- o Although less detailed than Nmap, Angry IP Scanner is useful for identifying active hosts and getting a rough overview of the target network.
- **Real-World Application**: A penetration tester may use Angry IP Scanner to perform a quick scan of a network to identify live hosts and target specific systems for further testing.

4. Nessus

Nessus is a widely-used vulnerability scanning tool that helps ethical hackers identify vulnerabilities on a target system. It checks for missing patches, outdated software versions, and configuration weaknesses.

- **Key Features**:
    - o **Vulnerability Scanning**: Nessus can scan for a wide range of known vulnerabilities, from misconfigured systems to software flaws.
    - o **Compliance Checks**: Nessus can check systems against security standards, such as PCI DSS or HIPAA, ensuring that systems meet regulatory requirements.

- o **Detailed Reporting**: Nessus provides detailed reports that help ethical hackers understand the severity of vulnerabilities and the necessary remediation steps.

- **How It Works**:
  - o Ethical hackers run Nessus on a target network to scan for vulnerabilities, such as missing patches or open ports that shouldn't be exposed.
  - o Nessus automatically compares systems against known vulnerability databases, providing a comprehensive list of potential security flaws.

- **Real-World Application**: In a corporate penetration test, Nessus can be used to scan a target's network for common vulnerabilities in their web servers, databases, or operating systems, enabling the tester to prioritize remediation efforts.

Techniques for Identifying Potential Vulnerabilities in a System

Once network scanning and enumeration are completed, the next step is to analyze the gathered information to identify potential vulnerabilities that could be exploited. Ethical hackers use a variety of techniques to assess the security of systems, applications, and networks, including manual and automated approaches.

1. Port Scanning and Service Fingerprinting

Port scanning is a critical technique for identifying open ports on a target system, which is essential for detecting services that may be vulnerable. By scanning a system's open ports, ethical hackers can pinpoint entry points for potential attacks.

- **Service Fingerprinting**: Once a service is discovered, ethical hackers attempt to determine the exact version of the service to check for known vulnerabilities. Tools like Nmap or Netcat can be used to capture service banners, which often reveal details about the software being used.
- **Real-World Example**: In a penetration test of a company's network, ethical hackers might scan for open ports on an external-facing server. Upon discovering an open FTP port, they could use service fingerprinting to identify that the server is running an outdated version of vsFTPd, which has a known vulnerability that allows remote code execution.

2. Vulnerability Scanning

Once services are identified, ethical hackers use automated vulnerability scanners to identify potential security flaws in the software running on those services. These tools check for missing patches, misconfigurations, weak passwords, or outdated software versions.

- **Real-World Example**: Ethical hackers using Nessus to scan a target system might identify an unpatched version of

Apache HTTP Server, which has a known vulnerability that allows attackers to execute arbitrary code. This discovery would allow the ethical hacker to exploit the vulnerability during the attack phase.

3. Enumerating Users and Shares

Enumeration is the process of gathering specific details about the target, such as user accounts, shared resources, and more. Ethical hackers often focus on identifying valuable user information, such as usernames, group memberships, or shared files, which can be useful for lateral movement and privilege escalation during the attack phase.

- **Tools**: Tools like **enum4linux** (for Linux-based systems) or **NBTscan** (for Windows) can be used to enumerate usernames and shared resources.
- **Real-World Example**: In a penetration test of a Windows environment, ethical hackers might enumerate a domain controller to discover a list of user accounts and shared files. This information could be used to launch brute-force attacks or gain further access to the network.

Scanning and enumeration are pivotal steps in the penetration testing process. Through the use of powerful tools like Nmap, Nessus, and Netcat, ethical hackers can map out networks, discover open ports, and identify services that could be vulnerable. By utilizing techniques like port scanning, vulnerability scanning, and enumeration, ethical hackers can pinpoint attack vectors and better understand the security posture of the target system. These techniques lay the groundwork for successful exploitation and remediation recommendations, which ultimately help organizations strengthen their defenses and reduce their exposure to cyber threats.

Chapter 7: Exploiting Vulnerabilities

What Are Vulnerabilities?

In the context of cybersecurity, **vulnerabilities** refer to weaknesses or flaws in a system, application, or network that can be exploited by attackers to gain unauthorized access, cause damage, or disrupt the functioning of the target. Vulnerabilities can arise due to various reasons, such as poor coding practices, misconfigurations, outdated software, or insufficient security controls.

A vulnerability typically results from a flaw in the design, implementation, or configuration of a system that compromises its security, confidentiality, integrity, or availability. These vulnerabilities can be exploited by attackers (or ethical hackers) to execute malicious actions, such as injecting malicious code, bypassing authentication mechanisms, or gaining unauthorized access to sensitive data.

Some common types of vulnerabilities include:

- **Software bugs**: Flaws in the code that can be exploited to perform unintended actions.
- **Configuration issues**: Misconfigurations of systems, networks, or applications that leave them open to attack.
- **Weak authentication**: Weak or improper authentication mechanisms that allow attackers to bypass security controls.

- **Unpatched software**: Systems running outdated versions of software or operating systems that have known vulnerabilities.

Understanding and identifying vulnerabilities is the first step in securing a system. Once vulnerabilities are discovered, ethical hackers use a variety of techniques to exploit these weaknesses to demonstrate how an attacker could compromise the system, all while working within legal boundaries and with the explicit permission of the system owner.

Exploit Techniques: Buffer Overflows, SQL Injection, XSS, etc.

Once vulnerabilities are identified during the reconnaissance, scanning, and enumeration phases, ethical hackers may attempt to exploit those weaknesses in the **attack phase**. Exploit techniques can vary widely, depending on the type of vulnerability present. Below are some of the most common exploitation techniques used by ethical hackers.

1. Buffer Overflow Exploits

A **buffer overflow** occurs when more data is written to a buffer (temporary storage in memory) than it can handle, causing the data to overwrite adjacent memory locations. This can lead to unpredictable behavior, crashes, or the execution of arbitrary code, allowing attackers to gain control over the target system.

- **How it works**: In a buffer overflow exploit, an attacker sends more data to a program's buffer than it can hold. If the program doesn't properly validate the input size, the extra data can overwrite the memory addresses stored next to the buffer. The attacker can use this to inject malicious code, which can then be executed with the same privileges as the vulnerable program.

- **Real-World Example**: In the **Morris Worm** attack of 1988, a buffer overflow vulnerability in the *sendmail* program on UNIX systems was exploited to spread a worm across thousands of machines. The worm used the buffer overflow to execute malicious code and infect the systems, leading to a significant internet outage.

- **Mitigation**: Proper input validation, using bounds checking, and adopting secure coding practices such as stack canaries and non-executable memory regions can help prevent buffer overflows.

2. SQL Injection (SQLi)

SQL injection is a type of attack where an attacker manipulates an SQL query by injecting malicious SQL code into the input fields of a web application. This allows the attacker to interact with the database and execute arbitrary queries, which can lead to unauthorized access to data, data modification, or even complete control over the database.

- **How it works**: SQL injection typically occurs when an application fails to properly validate user input and constructs SQL queries directly using user-supplied data. By inserting SQL syntax into input fields (such as login forms or search boxes), an attacker can manipulate the query's logic and execute commands that were never intended by the application developer.

- **Real-World Example**: One of the most infamous SQL injection attacks was the **Heartland Payment Systems** breach in 2008. Attackers exploited an SQL injection vulnerability in the company's payment system to gain access to sensitive financial data. The breach resulted in the theft of millions of credit card numbers.

- **Mitigation**: SQL injection can be mitigated by using prepared statements (parameterized queries), stored procedures, and strict input validation. Additionally, avoiding dynamic SQL queries and employing web application firewalls can help prevent SQLi attacks.

3. Cross-Site Scripting (XSS)

Cross-Site Scripting (XSS) is a vulnerability that allows attackers to inject malicious scripts into webpages viewed by other users. These scripts are typically written in JavaScript and can be used to steal cookies, hijack user sessions, deface websites, or perform other malicious activities.

- **How it works**: XSS occurs when an application includes untrusted data in the web page without proper validation or escaping. This allows an attacker to inject JavaScript into a webpage that is then executed by other users' browsers. There are different types of XSS, such as stored, reflected, and DOM-based XSS.

- **Real-World Example**: In **MySpace's Samy Worm (2005)**, an attacker injected a piece of JavaScript code into a MySpace profile. When users visited the profile, the script executed and caused the attacker's profile to become the most viewed profile on the platform. It also resulted in the hijacking of users' accounts and sessions.

- **Mitigation**: To prevent XSS, input validation and proper output encoding are essential. Web applications should sanitize user inputs and escape any data that will be included in HTML or JavaScript. Using Content Security Policy (CSP) headers and secure cookies also helps mitigate XSS risks.

4. Cross-Site Request Forgery (CSRF)

Cross-Site Request Forgery (CSRF) is an attack where an attacker tricks a user into performing an unintended action on a web application in which the user is authenticated. This can lead to the execution of unauthorized commands, such as changing the user's password, transferring funds, or submitting sensitive data.

- **How it works**: CSRF takes advantage of the fact that web applications often rely on cookies to authenticate users. If a user is logged into a site and then visits a malicious website, the attacker can trick the user's browser into sending a request to the legitimate site (e.g., a password change request) without the user's knowledge or consent.

- **Real-World Example**: In a **banking application** with weak CSRF protections, an attacker might trick an authenticated user into clicking on a link that initiates a funds transfer to the attacker's account, without the user's knowledge.

- **Mitigation**: To prevent CSRF, web applications should implement anti-CSRF tokens, which are unique values tied to each session or request. These tokens ensure that requests are only valid if they originate from the correct source. Additionally, same-origin policies and proper HTTP request methods (e.g., POST instead of GET) can help mitigate CSRF risks.

5. Privilege Escalation

Privilege escalation refers to the process by which an attacker gains higher levels of access or control over a system than they were initially granted. This can be achieved through exploiting software vulnerabilities, misconfigurations, or other weaknesses in the system.

- **How it works**: Attackers can escalate privileges in two ways: **vertical privilege escalation** (gaining higher-level access, such as from a regular user to an administrator) and **horizontal privilege escalation** (gaining access to resources or data meant for other users with the same level of access).

- **Real-World Example**: In the **Dirty COW** vulnerability (2016), a race condition in the Linux kernel allowed unprivileged users to escalate their privileges to root access, enabling them to modify system files and gain full control over the system.

- **Mitigation**: Privilege escalation can be prevented by enforcing the principle of least privilege (giving users only the permissions they need), using proper access control mechanisms, and applying security patches promptly.

Examples of Real-World Exploitation Scenarios

Exploiting vulnerabilities is often the turning point in a penetration test, where ethical hackers demonstrate how weaknesses in the system can be leveraged to achieve unauthorized access. Below are examples of real-world exploitation scenarios:

1. **Exploiting a Buffer Overflow**: In 2003, the **Blaster Worm** exploited a buffer overflow vulnerability in Microsoft

Windows to infect millions of computers. The worm exploited an unpatched vulnerability in the Windows DCOM (Distributed Component Object Model) service, allowing it to execute arbitrary code and spread across networks without user interaction.

2. **SQL Injection in Online Retailer**: In a well-known case, an online retailer was exploited via SQL injection in 2014. An attacker discovered an unvalidated input field on the site's search bar and used SQL injection to bypass the login page, gaining access to the retailer's database. This allowed the attacker to steal sensitive customer information, including credit card details.

3. **Cross-Site Scripting in Social Media Platforms**: In 2011, a **Twitter XSS vulnerability** allowed an attacker to inject malicious scripts into tweets. The attack was used to spread a worm that changed users' profiles and sent malicious links to their followers. Users who clicked on the links unknowingly spread the attack further.

4. **Privilege Escalation in Web Hosting**: In a case involving a popular web hosting company, an attacker was able to escalate privileges from a low-privileged user account to root access. By exploiting a vulnerability in the host's customer management system, the attacker gained control over all customer accounts, including the ability to install malware on hosted websites.

Exploiting vulnerabilities is the essence of penetration testing, as it demonstrates the impact of security weaknesses in real-world scenarios. By exploiting buffer overflows, SQL injection, XSS, and other vulnerabilities, ethical hackers help organizations understand how these weaknesses could be used by malicious hackers to compromise systems and data. Ethical hackers play a critical role in highlighting the importance of patching vulnerabilities, improving security practices, and maintaining a proactive approach to security.

Chapter 8: Social Engineering in Penetration Testing

Overview of Social Engineering Tactics

Social engineering is a critical aspect of ethical hacking and penetration testing, where human behavior is exploited rather than relying solely on technical vulnerabilities. It involves manipulating individuals into disclosing confidential information, granting unauthorized access, or performing actions that compromise security. Social engineering attacks exploit human psychology—such as trust, curiosity, fear, or urgency—to bypass traditional security measures like firewalls, encryption, or authentication systems.

Social engineering is often used in the early stages of an attack, helping attackers gather information, gain entry to secure systems, or escalate their privileges. In penetration testing, ethical hackers use social engineering tactics to simulate how real-world attackers might exploit human vulnerabilities to test an organization's overall security posture and improve awareness.

Since social engineering attacks involve human targets, they are highly effective and often difficult to defend against with technical security measures alone. Ethical hackers use social engineering as a tool to evaluate employees' awareness, organizational security policies, and vulnerability to manipulation. However, it is always important to get prior consent and adhere to ethical guidelines when conducting social engineering tests in penetration testing engagements.

Types of Social Engineering Attacks

There are several types of social engineering attacks, each designed to exploit different psychological triggers or behaviors. The most common forms of social engineering include **phishing**, **baiting**, and **pretexting**, though there are other variations as well. Below is a detailed explanation of these attack types and their characteristics.

1. Phishing

Phishing is one of the most common and widely recognized social engineering tactics. It involves sending fraudulent communications—typically via email—that appear to come from a trusted source. The goal of phishing is to trick the victim into providing sensitive information, such as usernames, passwords, credit card numbers, or other personal data.

- **How It Works**: In a phishing attack, the attacker typically impersonates a legitimate organization or trusted individual. The phishing email may contain a link to a fake website designed to look like a legitimate login page or instruct the victim to download a malicious attachment or file. Once the victim interacts with the content (e.g., clicks the link or downloads the attachment), the attacker can harvest sensitive data, install malware, or compromise the system.

- **Real-World Example**: A common phishing attack involves an attacker impersonating a financial institution (e.g., a bank) and sending an email claiming that the recipient's account has been compromised. The email prompts the recipient to click on a link and enter their login credentials to "verify their account." In reality, the link leads to a fake website where the attacker collects the login credentials and uses them for malicious purposes.

- **Mitigation**: Phishing can be mitigated through employee training on how to identify phishing emails, the use of multi-factor authentication (MFA), and email filtering solutions to detect suspicious messages.

2. Baiting

Baiting is a type of social engineering attack where the attacker offers something enticing, such as free software, music, or other valuable content, to lure victims into compromising their systems or security. The goal is to exploit the victim's curiosity or desire for something free, making it easier for the attacker to gain access to the system.

- **How It Works**: Baiting typically involves physical or digital bait. For instance, an attacker may leave an infected USB drive in a public place with the label "confidential" or "payroll information." If someone plugs the drive into their computer, it automatically installs malware or gives the attacker access to the victim's system. Digital baiting could involve fake offers for free downloads of software or pirated content that contain malware.

- **Real-World Example**: In the infamous **"Stuxnet"** attack, a USB drive containing a malware payload was used as a form of bait to infiltrate Iranian nuclear facilities. The attackers intentionally placed the infected USB drives in public areas, knowing that an employee would insert one into a machine, activating the malware and allowing the attackers to infiltrate the facility's systems.

- **Mitigation**: To mitigate baiting attacks, organizations should prohibit the use of unauthorized USB drives and external media, enforce strict access controls, and educate employees about the dangers of downloading unverified files or connecting unknown devices.

3. Pretexting

Pretexting is a form of social engineering where the attacker creates a fabricated scenario (the "pretext") to obtain information or access from the victim. This often involves impersonating someone of authority or a trusted individual, such as an IT administrator, company executive, or law enforcement officer. The attacker typically asks the victim to verify or provide sensitive information, such as passwords, bank details, or employee records, under the guise of legitimate business need.

- **How It Works**: In pretexting attacks, the attacker often uses detailed research to craft a convincing story. For example, they may call an employee in the finance department, pretending to be from the IT department and request the employee's credentials to "fix a system issue." Since the attack relies on trust, it can be particularly effective in organizational settings where employees may not question the authority of someone they believe to be from their own company.

- **Real-World Example**: A **telephone pretexting** attack might involve an attacker calling an employee at a company and pretending to be a manager or company representative. The attacker may claim that they need to confirm certain personal details for a company project and request sensitive information like Social Security numbers, passwords, or account numbers. If the employee falls for the pretext, they provide the attacker with valuable data.

- **Mitigation**: Pretexting can be mitigated by enforcing strict verification protocols and training employees to verify the identity of anyone requesting sensitive information. Additionally, limiting access to sensitive data and implementing multi-factor authentication can reduce the risk of falling for such attacks.

4. Vishing (Voice Phishing)

Vishing is a form of phishing that takes place over the phone. In a vishing attack, the attacker uses a phone call to impersonate a legitimate institution or authority figure, such as a bank representative, government official, or IT support technician, to deceive the victim into disclosing personal information or performing actions that compromise security.

- **How It Works**: Attackers often use caller ID spoofing to make their number appear as though it's coming from a trusted source. The victim may be asked to verify their identity or account details over the phone, which can lead to the disclosure of sensitive information such as passwords, credit card numbers, or social security numbers.

- **Real-World Example**: In a vishing attack, an attacker may call a bank customer and claim that there is a problem with their account. The attacker will ask the customer to confirm their account number, PIN, or other private details to resolve the issue. Once the victim provides this information, the attacker may use it for fraudulent purposes.

- **Mitigation**: To prevent vishing, individuals should be cautious when receiving unsolicited calls and avoid providing sensitive information over the phone.

Organizations can implement secure verification processes for phone-based interactions and educate employees and customers about vishing risks.

Case Studies Where Social Engineering Succeeded

1. **The Google and Facebook Scam (2013-2015)**: In a sophisticated social engineering attack, a hacker impersonated an Asian hardware supplier and tricked employees at both Google and Facebook into wiring over $100 million. The hacker used pretexting and forged emails to create fake invoices for equipment purchases. The scam was successful due to the attackers' careful research and the trust placed in the emails' apparent authenticity. Both companies were eventually able to recover most of the stolen funds, but the case highlights the power of pretexting in corporate environments.

2. **The Target Data Breach (2013)**: One of the largest data breaches in history, the **Target** breach, was facilitated by social engineering tactics. The attackers first gained access to Target's network by compromising a third-party vendor, an HVAC company, using a phishing attack. Once inside, the attackers used network vulnerabilities to access Target's payment systems and stole credit card information for over 40 million customers. This case underscores how social

engineering techniques, such as phishing, can serve as a gateway to more damaging attacks.

3. **The Ubiquiti Networks Attack (2015)**: In a case of pretexting, attackers impersonated the CEO of Ubiquiti Networks and instructed employees to transfer millions of dollars into a foreign bank account for an "overseas project." The employees were convinced by the pretext that the transfer was legitimate. The scam resulted in a loss of over $40 million. This case highlights how pretexting can be used to manipulate employees into acting against their better judgment when pressured by an authority figure.

Social engineering remains one of the most potent and effective attack vectors in the world of cybersecurity. Unlike traditional technical attacks, social engineering preys on human vulnerabilities—exploiting trust, fear, or curiosity to gain unauthorized access or sensitive information. Ethical hackers use social engineering techniques as part of penetration testing to evaluate how well an organization's employees can withstand manipulative tactics.

Phishing, baiting, pretexting, and vishing are just a few examples of how attackers manipulate individuals. By studying real-world case studies and understanding the tactics attackers use, organizations can develop better defense mechanisms, improve employee training, and implement strict verification protocols to reduce the risk of falling victim to social engineering attacks. Ultimately, awareness and preparation are key to defending against these deceptive tactics.

Chapter 9: Web Application Penetration Testing

How to Test Web Applications for Vulnerabilities

Web application penetration testing involves evaluating the security of web applications by identifying vulnerabilities that could potentially be exploited by attackers. Unlike traditional network penetration testing, which focuses on network and system-level vulnerabilities, web application testing specifically targets issues that can be found within the application code, web servers, and databases that host the application.

Testing web applications for vulnerabilities is essential to ensure the application is protected against common threats that can lead to data breaches, unauthorized access, or system compromise. The process of testing web applications involves several stages, including reconnaissance, vulnerability scanning, exploitation, and post-exploitation. Below is a detailed look at the steps involved in performing a web application penetration test:

1. Reconnaissance and Information Gathering

The first step in testing a web application is reconnaissance, where ethical hackers gather as much information as possible about the application, its components, and how it interacts with users and other systems. This can involve both **passive** and **active** reconnaissance.

- **Passive Reconnaissance**: Collecting publicly available information such as domain details, server configurations, HTTP headers, and SSL certificates. Tools like **WHOIS** lookups and **Google Dorking** can help uncover sensitive data about the application's infrastructure.
- **Active Reconnaissance**: Directly interacting with the web application to identify entry points, URLs, and potential attack surfaces. Tools like **Burp Suite**, **OWASP ZAP**, and **Nikto** are often used for active reconnaissance to map the application and detect weaknesses.

2. Scanning for Vulnerabilities

Once the reconnaissance phase is complete, the next step is to identify potential vulnerabilities in the web application. This can be done through automated tools or manual testing techniques.

- **Automated Scanning**: Tools like **OWASP ZAP, Burp Suite**, and **Acunetix** perform vulnerability scanning to identify common weaknesses, including SQL Injection, Cross-Site Scripting (XSS), and Cross-Site Request Forgery (CSRF). These tools automate the detection of security issues, making it easier to identify high-risk vulnerabilities quickly.

- **Manual Testing**: While automated tools are helpful, manual testing is often required to identify more complex vulnerabilities or logic flaws that automated scanners may miss. Manual testing might involve input validation checks, examining session management, testing for proper authentication mechanisms, and verifying access control rules.

3. Exploitation

Once vulnerabilities have been identified, the next step is to exploit them to verify their severity and demonstrate the potential impact on the application and its underlying systems. This step typically involves using the same tools and techniques as attackers might use to exploit the vulnerabilities.

- **SQL Injection**: Crafting malicious SQL queries to exploit vulnerabilities in the web application's database interaction.
- **Cross-Site Scripting (XSS)**: Injecting malicious JavaScript code into input fields or URLs to steal session cookies or redirect users to malicious sites.
- **Authentication Bypass**: Attempting to bypass the authentication mechanism (such as login forms or session management) to gain unauthorized access.

4. Post-Exploitation and Reporting

If an exploit is successful, the ethical hacker may attempt to escalate privileges, maintain access, or gather additional information from the compromised system. However, the primary goal of penetration testing is to report vulnerabilities and risks back to the organization with actionable recommendations for remediation.

A well-documented report should outline:

- A description of the vulnerabilities discovered.
- Evidence of how they were exploited (including screen captures or logs).
- A risk assessment based on the potential impact of each vulnerability.
- Detailed recommendations for mitigating or fixing the vulnerabilities.

Common Vulnerabilities in Web Applications

Web applications are often targets of cyberattacks due to their widespread use and complex interactions with databases, servers, and user input. Below are some of the most common vulnerabilities found in web applications that ethical hackers test for during penetration testing:

1. SQL Injection (SQLi)

SQL Injection occurs when an attacker is able to insert malicious SQL code into a web application's query. This typically happens when user inputs are not properly validated or sanitized before being used in SQL queries. SQLi can allow attackers to access, modify, or delete data in the database or even execute administrative commands.

- **Example**: An attacker may input the following in a login form:

  vbnet
  Copy
  ' OR 1=1 --

  This could cause the web application to return all user records from the database, allowing the attacker to log in without valid credentials.

- **Mitigation**: To prevent SQLi, web applications should use prepared statements (parameterized queries), validate and sanitize all user input, and implement least privilege access controls on databases.

2. Cross-Site Scripting (XSS)

Cross-Site Scripting (XSS) is a vulnerability where attackers inject malicious scripts (typically JavaScript) into web pages that are viewed by other users. This can allow attackers to steal session cookies, deface websites, or redirect users to malicious sites. XSS attacks can be divided into three types: stored, reflected, and DOM-based XSS.

- **Example**: In a stored XSS attack, an attacker might submit a malicious script in a comment form on a blog. When another user views the page, the script executes and steals their session cookie.

- **Mitigation**: Web applications should validate and sanitize all user input, implement Content Security Policy (CSP) headers, and escape output data to prevent script execution in the browser.

3. Cross-Site Request Forgery (CSRF)

Cross-Site Request Forgery (CSRF) is an attack where a user is tricked into executing unwanted actions on a website where they are authenticated. CSRF attacks typically exploit the trust that a website has in a user's browser, allowing the attacker to perform actions without the user's consent.

- **Example**: If a user is logged into a banking application, an attacker might trick the user into clicking a link that initiates a money transfer request without their knowledge.

- **Mitigation**: To prevent CSRF, web applications should implement anti-CSRF tokens that are unique to each session and included in every form submission. Additionally, using HTTP methods such as POST for sensitive actions and ensuring that session cookies are secure can help mitigate CSRF attacks.

4. Insecure Direct Object References (IDOR)

IDOR occurs when a web application exposes a reference to an internal object, such as a file, database record, or URL parameter, that can be manipulated by the user to access unauthorized resources. This type of vulnerability can allow attackers to bypass access controls and view or modify data that they should not have access to.

- **Example**: A user can change the URL from /account/view/12345 to /account/view/12346 and gain access to another user's account.
- **Mitigation**: To prevent IDOR, web applications should implement proper access control checks for all resources and avoid relying solely on user-supplied input to access objects.

5. Authentication and Session Management Vulnerabilities

Authentication and session management issues arise when web applications fail to securely manage user identities and sessions. Attackers can exploit weak or poorly implemented authentication mechanisms to gain unauthorized access to sensitive areas of an application.

- **Example**: If an application uses predictable session IDs or does not properly expire sessions, an attacker could hijack another user's session to impersonate them.

- **Mitigation**: Web applications should use secure session management practices, such as generating random session tokens, implementing multi-factor authentication (MFA), and ensuring that sessions are securely timed out after a period of inactivity.

Real-World Example of a Successful Web App Penetration Test

The eBay Incident (2014)

In 2014, a web application penetration test conducted on eBay uncovered several critical vulnerabilities that were eventually exploited by attackers. During the penetration testing engagement, ethical hackers discovered that eBay's website had several exposed entry points, including a **stored XSS vulnerability** in the product review system and an **SQL injection vulnerability** in the payment gateway.

- **Exploitation**: The ethical hackers successfully injected malicious JavaScript code into a product review, which was executed when other users viewed the product page. This allowed the attackers to steal users' session cookies and gain unauthorized access to their accounts. Additionally, the

SQLi vulnerability was used to extract sensitive user data from eBay's database, including credit card information.

- **Outcome**: The vulnerabilities were reported to eBay, which took immediate action to patch the issues. The company also implemented more stringent security measures, including improved input validation, tighter session management, and better security for payment systems. The penetration testing engagement helped eBay secure its platform and prevent further exploits.

Web application penetration testing is crucial for identifying vulnerabilities and strengthening the security of web-based systems. By using tools like Burp Suite, OWASP ZAP, and manual testing techniques, ethical hackers can uncover common vulnerabilities such as SQL Injection, XSS, and CSRF, which can be exploited to gain unauthorized access, steal data, or disrupt services. Real-world examples, such as the eBay incident, highlight the importance of web application security and demonstrate how penetration testing can help organizations identify and mitigate risks before they are exploited by malicious hackers. Through thorough testing and remediation, organizations can ensure that their web applications remain secure and resistant to attacks.

Chapter 10: Wireless Network Security

Understanding the Risks in Wireless Networks

Wireless networks, while offering convenience and flexibility, present unique security challenges compared to traditional wired networks. The very nature of wireless communication—transmitting data through the air—makes it susceptible to interception and unauthorized access. As organizations increasingly rely on wireless networks to connect devices and provide internet access, it's crucial to understand the inherent risks and how they can be mitigated.

Wireless networks use radio frequencies to transmit data between devices, such as routers, access points, and client devices (laptops, smartphones, etc.). While these networks offer mobility and ease of setup, they are exposed to several security threats that can potentially compromise sensitive information and disrupt services.

Some of the primary risks associated with wireless networks include:

1. Eavesdropping and Data Interception
Since wireless networks transmit data over radio waves, they are vulnerable to interception by attackers within range. Without proper encryption, attackers can capture data packets and gain access to sensitive information, such as login credentials, personal data, or

credit card details. Tools like Wireshark and Aircrack-ng can easily intercept and analyze unencrypted wireless traffic.

2. Rogue Access Points

Rogue access points are unauthorized devices that mimic legitimate Wi-Fi networks. These can be set up by attackers to lure users into connecting to them, thereby allowing the attacker to intercept and manipulate network traffic. Once connected, the attacker may also attempt to exploit vulnerabilities in the device or network.

3. Man-in-the-Middle (MITM) Attacks

In a MITM attack, an attacker intercepts and relays communications between two parties without their knowledge. In wireless networks, this could involve capturing data transmitted between a client and a legitimate access point. The attacker can then manipulate or steal the data, or even inject malicious code.

4. Denial of Service (DoS) Attacks

Wi-Fi networks are susceptible to DoS attacks that can disrupt network availability. Attackers can flood the network with excessive traffic or exploit vulnerabilities in the Wi-Fi protocol (such as deauthentication attacks) to force devices to disconnect from the network, causing service disruptions.

5. Weak Encryption and Authentication

Many wireless networks still rely on outdated encryption protocols like WEP (Wired Equivalent Privacy), which are easily cracked using modern tools. Even networks using WPA2 (Wi-Fi Protected Access) or WPA3 may be vulnerable if weak passwords or poor key management practices are used.

6. Network Spoofing

Attackers can spoof legitimate wireless networks, tricking users into connecting to them by using the same SSID (Service Set Identifier) as a trusted network. Once connected, attackers can launch further attacks or monitor network activity.

Penetration Testing Techniques for Wi-Fi Networks

Penetration testing of wireless networks involves simulating attacks to assess the security posture of Wi-Fi infrastructure. By using a variety of tools and techniques, ethical hackers can identify vulnerabilities, weak encryption methods, and areas where network security can be improved.

1. Network Discovery and Mapping

The first step in Wi-Fi penetration testing is to discover the wireless networks within range and map the network's topology. Ethical hackers use tools like **Kismet** or **Airodump-ng** to identify nearby access points, determine their signal strength, and collect information about the network configuration, including SSID, encryption type, and channel.

- **Tools**:

- ○ **Kismet**: A wireless network detector, sniffer, and intrusion detection system (IDS) that helps ethical hackers detect hidden networks, monitor traffic, and identify devices connected to the network.
- ○ **Airodump-ng**: A wireless packet sniffer that captures data packets, providing detailed information about networks and devices, including their MAC addresses, SSIDs, and encryption status.

2. Cracking WEP and WPA/WPA2 Keys

One of the most critical aspects of wireless network penetration testing is attempting to crack the encryption used to protect data on the network. Networks that use **WEP** (Wired Equivalent Privacy) are particularly vulnerable, as WEP can be cracked quickly with tools like **Aircrack-ng** or **Wireshark**. Networks using **WPA** (Wi-Fi Protected Access) or **WPA2** are more secure but still susceptible to brute-force or dictionary attacks, especially if weak passwords are used.

- **Tools**:
  - ○ **Aircrack-ng**: A suite of tools used to crack WEP and WPA-PSK (Pre-Shared Key) encryption. It captures packets and uses them to guess the key through brute-force or dictionary attacks.

- ○ **Cowpatty**: A password-cracking tool for WPA and WPA2 networks that uses a pre-shared key for brute-forcing.

3. Man-in-the-Middle (MITM) Attacks

MITM attacks in wireless networks involve intercepting communication between devices and access points. Ethical hackers use MITM techniques to intercept data and attempt to manipulate or steal sensitive information. Tools like **Ettercap** and **Wireshark** are commonly used to perform MITM attacks in wireless environments.

- **Tools**:
    - ○ **Ettercap**: A comprehensive suite for MITM attacks that allows the attacker to intercept, modify, and inject malicious data into network communications.
    - ○ **Wireshark**: A network protocol analyzer that can capture and analyze wireless packets, revealing sensitive information like usernames, passwords, and session cookies.

4. Rogue Access Point and Evil Twin Attacks

Ethical hackers may set up rogue access points or use evil twin attacks to simulate malicious hotspots. By mimicking a trusted Wi-Fi network, they can observe and intercept traffic from unsuspecting users who connect to the rogue access point. Tools like **Airbase-ng** or **Karma** are commonly used to create rogue access points.

- **Tools**:
  - ○ **Airbase-ng**: A tool within the Aircrack-ng suite that allows attackers to create rogue access points that mimic legitimate networks.
  - ○ **Karma**: A tool that automatically responds to probe requests from Wi-Fi-enabled devices, enticing them to connect to the fake access point.

5. Deauthentication Attacks

Deauthentication attacks are a type of DoS attack that forces devices to disconnect from the access point. By flooding the network with deauthentication packets, an attacker can disrupt legitimate communication between devices and the router. This attack is often used to force devices to reconnect to the attacker's rogue access point or to prevent access to the network.

- **Tools**:
  - ○ **MDK3**: A tool that can be used to launch deauthentication and other DoS attacks against Wi-Fi networks.
  - ○ **Aircrack-ng**: Also supports deauthentication attacks as part of its toolkit for testing the availability and robustness of wireless networks.

6. Wi-Fi Protected Setup (WPS) Brute-Force Attacks

WPS is a feature designed to simplify the process of connecting devices to a wireless network. However, it has been found to have serious security flaws, especially in networks that use a PIN for authentication. Ethical hackers can exploit these vulnerabilities by launching brute-force attacks against WPS-enabled routers to obtain the Wi-Fi password.

- **Tools**:
  - o **Reaver**: A tool that allows attackers to brute-force WPS PINs on vulnerable routers, bypassing the standard WPA/WPA2 security and gaining access to the network.

Real-World Attack Examples on Wi-Fi Networks

1. **The Stuxnet Worm (2010)**: While not exclusively a Wi-Fi attack, Stuxnet is one of the most sophisticated and well-known cyberattacks that leveraged wireless network vulnerabilities to spread. In this case, a USB drive infected with the worm was used to gain access to Iranian nuclear facilities. The worm then spread through the facility's networks, including their Wi-Fi systems, exploiting vulnerabilities to damage equipment. This attack demonstrated the importance of securing not only wired networks but also wireless communications.

2. **The Crack of WEP Encryption (2000s)**: WEP (Wired Equivalent Privacy) was once the standard encryption for wireless networks but was found to have serious vulnerabilities. In the early 2000s, researchers discovered that WEP could be cracked in a matter of minutes using tools like **Aircrack-ng** and **Kismet**. Attackers could easily intercept and decrypt network traffic, exposing sensitive information like passwords and email content. This led to widespread adoption of more secure protocols like WPA and WPA2.

3. **The "Evil Twin" Attack at Starbucks (2014)**: A well-known case of a rogue access point attack took place at a Starbucks in the United States. A hacker set up an evil twin access point that mimicked the Starbucks Wi-Fi network. Unsuspecting customers connected to the fake network, believing it to be legitimate. Once connected, the attacker was able to monitor their web traffic, steal sensitive data like login credentials, and launch malware attacks on their devices.

4. **KRACK Attack (2017)**: The **KRACK (Key Reinstallation Attack)** vulnerability exploited weaknesses in the WPA2 protocol, which was supposed to secure Wi-Fi networks. Attackers could use this vulnerability to intercept and decrypt network traffic between Wi-Fi devices and access points, exposing sensitive data. This flaw affected nearly

every Wi-Fi-enabled device in the world, and although it required the attacker to be within range of the target network, it showcased how even widely adopted security protocols could have vulnerabilities.

Wireless network security is an essential aspect of modern cybersecurity, as more organizations rely on Wi-Fi networks to provide flexibility and mobility. However, the inherent risks associated with wireless communication require proactive measures to secure these networks from various attacks, including eavesdropping, rogue access points, MITM attacks, and deauthentication attacks. Penetration testing of wireless networks helps organizations identify vulnerabilities and assess their defenses against potential threats.

By using tools like **Aircrack-ng**, **Kismet**, and **Reaver**, ethical hackers can test the robustness of Wi-Fi networks, uncover vulnerabilities, and provide actionable recommendations for securing wireless communications. Understanding the risks and implementing appropriate security measures—such as strong encryption, secure authentication methods, and regular network monitoring—is essential to maintaining a secure wireless environment in today's interconnected world.

Chapter 11: Network Penetration Testing

The Importance of Network Penetration Testing

Network penetration testing (network pentesting) is a proactive approach to identifying and mitigating security vulnerabilities within an organization's network infrastructure. It involves simulating real-world attacks to test the effectiveness of an organization's network defenses, identify weaknesses, and provide actionable recommendations for improvement. Network pentesting is essential for organizations seeking to secure their network systems from potential cyberattacks, as it helps assess the strength of security measures and identify vulnerabilities before they can be exploited by malicious actors.

Network penetration testing is critical for several reasons:

1. **Identifying Vulnerabilities**: Networks are complex, with multiple devices, protocols, and configurations that can contain vulnerabilities. These vulnerabilities, if left unchecked, can become gateways for attackers to compromise sensitive data or disrupt services. Network pentesting helps identify these vulnerabilities in a controlled environment.

2. **Assessing Network Security Posture**: Network penetration testing allows organizations to assess their overall security

posture. By testing the network's defenses, organizations can gain insight into how well their firewalls, intrusion detection/prevention systems (IDS/IPS), and other security measures are working.

3. **Simulating Real-World Attacks**: A key benefit of network pentesting is the ability to simulate real-world attacks, such as Distributed Denial of Service (DDoS), man-in-the-middle (MITM), and privilege escalation attacks, to see how well the network can defend against them. This helps organizations prepare for actual attacks and minimize the damage caused by breaches.

4. **Ensuring Compliance**: Many organizations are required to meet industry-specific compliance regulations such as PCI DSS, HIPAA, and GDPR. Regular network penetration testing helps ensure compliance with these regulations by identifying and addressing security gaps that could lead to non-compliance.

5. **Protecting Against Insider Threats**: While external threats are often the focus of penetration testing, internal threats pose a significant risk as well. Network pentesting can help identify potential vulnerabilities that could be exploited by insiders, whether they are malicious actors or employees who inadvertently compromise security.

6. **Mitigating Data Breaches**: Network breaches can lead to serious consequences, including data theft, reputational

damage, and financial losses. By conducting penetration tests regularly, organizations can detect vulnerabilities before they are exploited, minimizing the risk of a breach and ensuring sensitive data remains secure.

Tools and Techniques Used to Test Network Security

Network penetration testing involves a variety of tools and techniques that are used to assess the security of a network's devices, services, and protocols. These tools can help ethical hackers scan for vulnerabilities, exploit weaknesses, and analyze the network traffic to identify attack vectors.

1. Nmap (Network Mapper)

Nmap is a powerful and widely used open-source tool for network exploration and vulnerability scanning. It allows ethical hackers to map out a network, identify live hosts, and discover open ports and services running on those hosts.

- **Key Features**:
    - **Host Discovery**: Nmap can quickly identify live hosts on a network by sending ping requests or other probes.
    - **Port Scanning**: It scans for open ports on the target network and identifies which services are running on those ports.

- **Service and Version Detection**: Nmap can identify the versions of services running on open ports, providing valuable information to ethical hackers for finding vulnerabilities associated with outdated software.

- **OS Detection**: Nmap can often detect the operating system of a target machine based on its responses to network traffic.

- **Usage**: Ethical hackers use Nmap to scan for open ports, services, and potential attack surfaces in a network. The information gathered helps identify the next steps in testing the network's security measures.

2. Wireshark

Wireshark is a widely used network protocol analyzer that allows ethical hackers to capture and analyze network traffic in real-time. By examining the data packets transmitted over a network, ethical hackers can identify malicious activity, network misconfigurations, or insecure communication protocols.

- **Key Features**:
  - **Packet Capture**: Wireshark captures network traffic and allows ethical hackers to inspect the contents of each packet transmitted over the network.

- o **Protocol Analysis**: Wireshark supports analysis of hundreds of network protocols, such as TCP, UDP, HTTP, DNS, and more.
- o **Traffic Filtering**: It provides advanced filtering options to focus on specific traffic, such as communication between certain devices or traffic on specific ports.
- **Usage**: Ethical hackers use Wireshark to analyze network traffic during penetration tests to identify security issues like unencrypted passwords, unauthorized data transmission, or potential MITM attacks.

3. Metasploit Framework

The *Metasploit Framework* is one of the most popular and powerful tools for exploiting vulnerabilities in a network. It provides a wide range of pre-built exploits and payloads that can be used to gain access to vulnerable systems.

- **Key Features**:
  - o **Exploit Development**: Metasploit allows ethical hackers to develop or use pre-existing exploits to take advantage of vulnerabilities found in a network.
  - o **Payloads**: It provides various payloads that allow ethical hackers to gain control over compromised systems, escalate privileges, or gather sensitive information.

- o **Post-Exploitation**: After exploiting a vulnerability, Metasploit provides tools for maintaining access and gathering more data from the compromised system.
- **Usage**: Ethical hackers use Metasploit to automate the exploitation of vulnerabilities identified during the network pentesting process. It allows them to test real-world attack scenarios and demonstrate how an attacker could breach a network.

4. Nessus

Nessus is a widely used vulnerability scanner that helps ethical hackers detect weaknesses in network configurations, operating systems, and applications. It scans for known vulnerabilities, unpatched software, misconfigurations, and weak access controls.

- **Key Features**:
  - o **Vulnerability Scanning**: Nessus scans for thousands of vulnerabilities in network systems, including missing patches, outdated software, and insecure configurations.
  - o **Compliance Checks**: It helps ensure that networks comply with industry standards and regulatory requirements such as PCI DSS, HIPAA, and others.
  - o **Detailed Reporting**: Nessus generates detailed reports that provide a comprehensive overview of the

vulnerabilities identified, their severity, and recommendations for remediation.

- **Usage**: Ethical hackers use Nessus to conduct vulnerability assessments on network systems to identify weaknesses before they can be exploited by attackers.

5. Aircrack-ng

Aircrack-ng is a suite of tools used for testing the security of Wi-Fi networks. It is designed to assess the strength of encryption protocols like WEP, WPA, and WPA2 and helps ethical hackers identify weaknesses in wireless network security.

- **Key Features**:
  - **Packet Sniffing**: Aircrack-ng allows ethical hackers to capture packets from wireless networks, which can be analyzed to gather information about the network and its security settings.
  - **Cracking WEP and WPA Keys**: It includes tools for cracking WEP and WPA-PSK encryption, using techniques like brute-force and dictionary attacks.
- **Usage**: Ethical hackers use Aircrack-ng to test the security of Wi-Fi networks by attempting to decrypt traffic or crack the encryption key, helping organizations strengthen their wireless security protocols.

Examples of Network-Based Attacks and How to Mitigate Them

Network-based attacks are an ever-present threat to organizations, and ethical hackers must be able to simulate and defend against these attacks during penetration testing engagements. Below are some common network-based attacks and strategies for mitigating them.

1. Man-in-the-Middle (MITM) Attack

In a MITM attack, an attacker intercepts and relays communications between two parties, often without their knowledge. The attacker can modify or inject malicious data into the communication stream, steal sensitive information, or impersonate one of the parties.

- **Real-World Example**: In a MITM attack targeting a corporate VPN, an attacker could intercept and alter sensitive communications between an employee and the corporate network, potentially exfiltrating login credentials or altering files being transferred.
- **Mitigation**:
  - Use **strong encryption** protocols such as TLS or HTTPS for secure communication.
  - Implement **mutual authentication** to ensure both parties are who they claim to be.
  - Enforce the use of **VPNs** with strong encryption to protect communications on public networks.

2. Denial of Service (DoS) and Distributed Denial of Service (DDoS)

DoS and DDoS attacks aim to overwhelm a target system or network with excessive traffic, rendering it inaccessible to legitimate users. In a DDoS attack, the attacker uses a network of compromised devices (a botnet) to launch the attack.

- **Real-World Example**: The 2016 **Dyn DDoS attack** targeted a popular DNS service provider, causing widespread disruption to major websites such as Twitter, Reddit, and Spotify. The attack used a botnet made up of IoT devices that flooded Dyn's servers with traffic, causing outages across the internet.
- **Mitigation**:
  - Implement **rate limiting** and **traffic filtering** to detect and block malicious traffic.
  - Use **Content Delivery Networks (CDNs)** and **load balancing** to distribute traffic and absorb high volumes of legitimate and malicious requests.
  - Employ **intrusion detection systems (IDS)** to detect and mitigate DDoS attacks in real-time.

3. Privilege Escalation

Privilege escalation occurs when an attacker gains elevated access to a system, allowing them to perform actions they are not authorized to do. Privilege escalation can occur through exploiting vulnerabilities, weak configurations, or inadequate access controls.

- **Real-World Example**: The **Dirty COW** vulnerability (2016) allowed unprivileged users on Linux systems to escalate their privileges to root, potentially allowing attackers to modify system files or install malware.
- **Mitigation**:
  - o Use the principle of **least privilege** to ensure that users and applications only have the minimum permissions necessary to perform their tasks.
  - o Regularly apply **security patches** and updates to fix known vulnerabilities.
  - o Implement **multi-factor authentication (MFA)** and enforce strong password policies to reduce the risk of unauthorized access.

Network penetration testing is a critical aspect of maintaining a secure network infrastructure. By using tools like **Nmap**, **Wireshark**, **Metasploit**, and **Nessus**, ethical hackers can simulate real-world attacks, identify vulnerabilities, and provide actionable recommendations for improving network security. Understanding common network-based attacks such as MITM, DoS, and privilege escalation, and knowing how to mitigate them, is essential for organizations to defend against emerging cyber threats and ensure the confidentiality, integrity, and availability of their networks.

Chapter 12: Operating System and Server Penetration Testing

Testing Security in Different Operating Systems (Windows, Linux)

Operating system (OS) and server security testing is an essential part of penetration testing. Every OS has its own strengths and weaknesses, and security testing requires specific tools and techniques tailored to the operating system in question. Windows and Linux are the two most commonly used operating systems in enterprise environments, and ethical hackers must understand how to test security on both.

1. Windows Security Testing

Windows operating systems, particularly in enterprise environments, are frequent targets for cyberattacks due to their wide use and often complex configuration. Security testing on Windows systems typically involves identifying common vulnerabilities such as misconfigurations, weak password policies, and unpatched software.

- **Key Areas of Windows Security Testing**:
  - **User Accounts and Privileges**: Testing the strength of user account controls, password policies, and group memberships. Many Windows environments use Active Directory (AD) to manage users and

permissions, so testing should include checking for weak or reused passwords, misconfigured permissions, and unauthorized user accounts.

o **File System Security**: Checking for insecure file permissions, unprotected sensitive data, and weak encryption settings.

o **Windows Services**: Evaluating which services are running on the system, particularly those with unnecessary or default configurations, which may be exploitable.

o **Vulnerabilities and Patches**: Ensuring that the operating system and installed software are up-to-date with the latest security patches. Unpatched systems are vulnerable to known exploits that can be easily exploited by attackers.

o **Registry Security**: The Windows registry is a key area for testing as misconfigured settings can expose the system to attacks.

- **Tools for Windows Security Testing**:

o **Nessus**: Used to scan for known vulnerabilities in Windows systems, including missing patches and insecure configurations.

o **Metasploit**: Can be used to exploit known vulnerabilities in Windows operating systems and applications.

- o **Cain and Abel**: A tool used for password cracking and sniffing network traffic to identify weak passwords.
- o **Netcat**: Often used to create reverse shells on compromised systems.

2. Linux Security Testing

Linux is widely used for servers and workstations in corporate environments. While Linux is often considered more secure than Windows due to its open-source nature and better patch management, it is still vulnerable to a range of security issues, including weak user controls, unpatched software, and configuration flaws.

- **Key Areas of Linux Security Testing**:
  - o **File Permissions**: Linux file permissions are a critical aspect of security. Ethical hackers will test if the file system is properly segmented, ensuring that files containing sensitive information have restricted access. Misconfigured permissions can provide unauthorized access to sensitive files.
  - o **Sudo and Root Privileges**: Privilege escalation tests should be conducted to identify potential vulnerabilities that could allow unprivileged users to gain root access, often using weak sudo configurations or unpatched exploits.

- o **Unnecessary Services**: Testing should identify unnecessary or unused services running on the system, as these can present attack vectors. Services such as SSH, FTP, and Apache should only be running if necessary and configured securely.

- o **Vulnerabilities and Patches**: Ensuring the system is running the latest security patches and there are no known vulnerabilities on the server.

- o **Authentication**: Testing for weaknesses in authentication mechanisms, including the use of default credentials and weak passwords.

- **Tools for Linux Security Testing**:
  - o **Nmap**: Used to discover open ports and services running on Linux machines.

  - o **Lynis**: A security auditing tool for Linux that performs system hardening and vulnerability assessments.

  - o **John the Ripper**: A popular password cracking tool used to identify weak passwords on Linux systems.

  - o **Metasploit**: Useful for exploiting vulnerabilities on Linux systems to test for security flaws.

  - o **Nikto**: Used for web server scanning to detect vulnerabilities in web applications hosted on Linux-based servers.

Server Security Testing and Techniques to Find Flaws

Servers are a central component of any IT infrastructure, and they often hold sensitive information, such as databases, web applications, and internal communications. Testing the security of servers is therefore critical in identifying weaknesses that could lead to unauthorized access, data leaks, or service disruptions.

1. Server Configuration Testing

The first step in server security testing is to assess its configuration. Misconfigurations in services, software, and firewall settings can open servers up to attacks. A server penetration test often starts by identifying unnecessary services and configurations that could be exploited.

- **Key Areas**:
  - ○ **Firewall Configuration**: Testing for open ports that should not be exposed to the internet.
  - ○ **Service Configuration**: Identifying unnecessary services (e.g., FTP, Telnet) that are running on the server and may expose it to vulnerabilities.
  - ○ **Security Policies**: Checking for misconfigurations in security policies related to user access control, password policies, and access to sensitive resources.

2. Authentication and Access Control

Inadequate authentication methods or improper access controls can allow attackers to gain unauthorized access to sensitive parts of the server. Ethical hackers test for weak authentication mechanisms, such as simple passwords, poor session management, and insecure communication channels (e.g., HTTP instead of HTTPS).

- **Key Areas**:
    - o **Brute Force Attacks**: Attempting to gain unauthorized access to user accounts or administrative accounts by trying various username and password combinations.
    - o **Credential Stuffing**: Using previously breached usernames and passwords to attempt access.
    - o **Session Hijacking**: Testing the server for weaknesses in session management that could allow attackers to steal or guess session tokens.

3. Vulnerability Scanning and Exploitation

Once the server's configuration and access controls are tested, ethical hackers use vulnerability scanning tools to detect known vulnerabilities in the server's software stack. Servers often run multiple services, such as web servers, databases, and mail servers, each of which could have vulnerabilities that need to be addressed.

- **Key Areas**:

o **Web Server Vulnerabilities**: Identifying flaws in the web server software (e.g., Apache, Nginx, IIS) or the web application running on it (e.g., SQL injection, XSS).

o **Operating System Vulnerabilities**: Testing for vulnerabilities in the server's OS that could allow an attacker to gain control over the server.

o **Database Vulnerabilities**: Testing for insecure database configurations, weak passwords, or vulnerabilities such as SQL injection.

4. Privilege Escalation

Privilege escalation tests are essential for assessing whether users with limited access can gain higher-level access (e.g., root, admin) by exploiting vulnerabilities in the server's operating system or configuration. This step typically involves attempting to break out of user roles and gain full control of the server.

- **Tools**: Privilege escalation tools like **Linux Exploit Suggester** and **Windows Exploit Suggester** help ethical hackers identify potential vulnerabilities that may allow for privilege escalation.

Real-World Server Penetration Testing Scenario

The Sony PlayStation Network (PSN) Breach (2011)

One of the most significant real-world examples of a server penetration test scenario that went wrong was the 2011 **Sony PlayStation Network (PSN) breach**. While this was not a direct penetration test, it serves as a cautionary tale of how poor security measures on web servers and databases can lead to massive data breaches.

- **Attack Overview**: The breach occurred when attackers exploited vulnerabilities in Sony's web servers, which hosted the PlayStation Network and Sony Online Entertainment services. The attackers exploited weaknesses in outdated software, misconfigured servers, and poor network segmentation to gain access to Sony's internal systems. Once inside, the attackers were able to steal personal data, including 77 million accounts, credit card details, and other sensitive information.
- **Vulnerabilities**:
  - **Outdated Software**: Sony had not applied critical security patches to their servers, making them vulnerable to attacks.
  - **Weak Network Segmentation**: Attackers were able to move laterally within the network once they compromised the web server, ultimately gaining access to sensitive data.

- ○ **Inadequate Logging and Monitoring**: Sony's systems lacked adequate monitoring to detect the attack in real time, allowing the attackers to remain undetected for a long time.
- **Mitigation Lessons**:
  - ○ **Regular Software Updates and Patching**: It is critical to keep all server software and applications up to date with the latest security patches.
  - ○ **Network Segmentation**: Proper network segmentation can help prevent attackers from moving laterally within the network once they compromise one server.
  - ○ **Intrusion Detection and Monitoring**: Effective logging and monitoring systems can help detect unusual activity in real-time, allowing quicker responses to potential threats.

Penetration testing on operating systems and servers is essential for identifying vulnerabilities that could compromise the security of critical infrastructure. Windows and Linux operating systems require tailored testing approaches, each with its own set of tools and techniques to assess security. Server security testing focuses on configuration, access control, vulnerability scanning, and privilege escalation, all of which are critical to maintaining a secure environment. Real-world examples, such as the Sony PSN breach, highlight the importance of securing servers and applying regular patching and monitoring practices to mitigate potential attacks. Through comprehensive testing and remediation, organizations can protect their systems from the growing array of cyber threats that target operating systems and servers.

Chapter 13: Password Cracking and Security

Methods of Password Cracking (Brute Force, Dictionary Attacks, Rainbow Tables)

Passwords are one of the most fundamental aspects of cybersecurity, serving as the primary defense mechanism for user accounts, network access, and encrypted data. However, passwords are only as strong as the methods used to create and protect them. Attackers frequently attempt to crack passwords using various techniques, exploiting weak or commonly used passwords to gain unauthorized access to systems and data.

1. Brute Force Attacks

A **brute force attack** is one of the most straightforward methods of password cracking. In a brute force attack, an attacker systematically tries every possible combination of characters until the correct password is found. The effectiveness of this method depends on the length and complexity of the password. Shorter and simpler passwords are easier to crack with brute force attacks, while longer and more complex passwords can take much longer to crack.

- **How it Works**: Brute force attacks rely on computational power to guess passwords. Tools like **John the Ripper** and **Hydra** automate the process of trying different combinations of characters. For example, if a password is eight characters long, the brute force attack will try every possible combination of those eight characters, from "a" to "z", "A" to "Z", and special characters.

- **Real-World Example**: The 2014 **RockYou** breach exposed the password data of over 32 million users. A large portion of the passwords were weak and easily cracked via brute force methods, with many users opting for simple passwords like "123456" or "password".

- **Mitigation**: To defend against brute force attacks, it's critical to use long, complex passwords and employ account lockout mechanisms after a certain number of failed login attempts. **Multi-factor authentication (MFA)** can also significantly reduce the risk by adding an additional layer of security.

2. Dictionary Attacks

A **dictionary attack** is a more efficient method than brute force. It involves trying a predefined list of common passwords or words from a dictionary. Rather than attempting every possible character combination, dictionary attacks focus on common, easy-to-guess passwords and words typically used by people. These attacks can be significantly faster than brute force since they attempt words and phrases likely to be used.

- **How it Works**: In a dictionary attack, the attacker uses a tool to try each word in a list (dictionary file). This list may include common passwords like "password", "123456", or "qwerty", along with variations of those words, such as capitalizing the first letter or appending numbers.

- **Real-World Example**: The **LinkedIn** breach of 2012 exposed millions of password hashes. Many of the exposed passwords were simple dictionary words, making it easy for attackers to use dictionary-based cracking techniques to quickly find matches.

- **Mitigation**: To protect against dictionary attacks, users should avoid using simple, common words or variations of them. Implementing **password policies** that require the use of uppercase and lowercase letters, numbers, and special characters can increase password complexity. Again, **multi-factor authentication (MFA)** is a strong defense mechanism against this type of attack.

3. Rainbow Tables

Rainbow tables are precomputed tables of hash values used to reverse cryptographic hash functions, allowing attackers to quickly look up the plain text of hashed passwords. Rather than trying to compute the hash of each potential password guess in real-time (as in brute force or dictionary attacks), rainbow tables contain a large collection of precomputed hash values for common passwords and their variations.

- **How it Works**: When a password is hashed (using algorithms like MD5, SHA-1, or SHA-256), it becomes a fixed-length string of characters. Rainbow tables map these hashes to their corresponding plaintext passwords. The attacker can use the precomputed table to find the original password that corresponds to a specific hash.

- **Real-World Example**: Rainbow tables have been used to crack weakly hashed passwords that do not utilize proper **salting** techniques. In some older breaches, such as the **Adobe** breach in 2013, attackers used rainbow tables to crack passwords that were stored with weak hashes.

- **Mitigation**: To prevent rainbow table attacks, it is critical to use **salting** when hashing passwords. A salt is a random value added to the password before hashing, making it unique and much harder to crack using precomputed tables. Additionally, more secure hashing algorithms such as **bcrypt** or **Argon2** can slow down the process of brute force and rainbow table attacks by introducing computational complexity.

Best Practices for Secure Passwords

To ensure that passwords remain secure and resistant to cracking attempts, it's essential to follow best practices for password creation and management. Below are some of the most effective strategies for improving password security:

1. Use Strong and Complex Passwords

- **Length and Complexity**: Strong passwords should be at least 12-16 characters long and contain a mix of uppercase and lowercase letters, numbers, and special characters. Passwords should not use easily guessable information, such as names, birthdates, or simple words.
- **Passphrases**: Instead of a single word, use a passphrase—a combination of random words or a sentence that is difficult to guess but easy to remember. For example, "BlueDinosaur7JumpsHigh!" is a strong passphrase.

2. Avoid Password Reuse

Reusing passwords across multiple accounts increases the risk that if one account is compromised, attackers can use the same password to access other accounts. Use a **password manager** to generate and store unique, complex passwords for each service.

3. Implement Multi-Factor Authentication (MFA)

Multi-factor authentication (MFA) adds an additional layer of security by requiring users to verify their identity using more than just a password. This typically involves something the user knows (a password) and something the user has (a one-time code sent via SMS or generated by an authenticator app).

- **Real-World Example**: Many organizations, including Google, Facebook, and banks, now require MFA for accessing accounts to mitigate the risks associated with stolen or weak passwords.

4. Regular Password Updates

Encourage users to regularly update passwords, especially when a breach is detected or suspected. Set policies to prompt password changes periodically but avoid excessive frequency that leads to users creating weaker passwords.

5. Password Hashing and Salting

When storing passwords in a database, always hash passwords using a strong hashing algorithm (e.g., bcrypt, Argon2) and use a unique **salt** for each password. This makes it more difficult for attackers to use rainbow tables and precomputed hashes to crack the passwords.

6. Educate Users about Phishing and Social Engineering

Even the strongest passwords can be compromised through social engineering tactics, such as phishing. Users should be trained to recognize phishing attempts and suspicious activity and to avoid clicking on links or downloading attachments from untrusted sources.

Case Studies of Password-Related Breaches

Several high-profile breaches have occurred due to poor password management practices, illustrating the importance of implementing secure password policies.

1. The LinkedIn Breach (2012)

In 2012, LinkedIn suffered a major breach where 6.5 million user passwords were stolen and posted on a Russian hacker forum. The passwords were stored in a weakly hashed format (using the MD5 algorithm), and many users had chosen weak passwords or reused passwords across multiple platforms. As a result, attackers were able to use the exposed passwords to gain access to other accounts.

- **Impact**: The breach affected millions of LinkedIn users and led to a widespread campaign of account hijacking. In response, LinkedIn strengthened its password storage mechanisms, including implementing stronger encryption methods and urging users to change their passwords.
- **Lessons Learned**: This breach underscores the importance of using strong hashing algorithms like bcrypt or Argon2 and never storing passwords in plaintext or weakly hashed formats.

2. The Adobe Breach (2013)

In 2013, Adobe suffered a massive data breach that exposed over 150 million user accounts. The stolen data included usernames, email addresses, and hashed passwords. Adobe had used an outdated hashing algorithm (AES-128), which was easily cracked with rainbow tables. Additionally, many users had weak passwords or reused them across multiple accounts.

- **Impact**: The breach led to widespread password resetting, user account lockouts, and the leakage of sensitive customer information, including credit card details.
- **Lessons Learned**: The breach highlighted the importance of using strong, modern hashing algorithms (e.g., bcrypt) and implementing salting to make hashed passwords harder to crack.

3. The Yahoo Breach (2013-2014)

The Yahoo data breach, which was revealed in 2016, compromised over 3 billion user accounts, making it one of the largest breaches in history. The attackers used passwords stored in an outdated hashing format (MD5) and exploited weak password management practices.

- **Impact**: The breach exposed sensitive user data, including passwords, security questions, and other personal information. Attackers were able to use the compromised data for account takeovers and identity theft.

- **Lessons Learned**: The breach reinforced the need for password hashing best practices, multi-factor authentication, and regular security audits to prevent large-scale attacks.

Password security remains one of the most critical aspects of protecting online accounts, sensitive data, and systems. While password cracking techniques such as brute force, dictionary attacks, and rainbow tables are commonly used by attackers, adopting best practices for creating, storing, and managing passwords can significantly reduce the risk of a breach. Using strong passwords, employing multi-factor authentication, and utilizing proper password hashing and salting techniques can protect against the majority of password-based attacks. Additionally, educating users on the dangers of weak passwords and phishing can further mitigate the risk of unauthorized access and data breaches.

Chapter 14: Exploiting and Securing Web Servers

Web Server Vulnerabilities (Apache, IIS)

Web servers are critical components in any organization's IT infrastructure, serving as the gateway for serving web content to users. However, they are often prime targets for attackers due to the sensitive data they process and their exposure to the public internet. The two most widely used web server software packages—**Apache** and **Internet Information Services (IIS)**—each have their own specific vulnerabilities and security considerations.

1. Apache Web Server Vulnerabilities

Apache is an open-source web server that runs on Unix-based systems (like Linux) and Windows. As one of the most popular web servers globally, it is frequently targeted by attackers. Apache is prone to a variety of security vulnerabilities, many of which can be exploited if the server is not configured correctly or if it is running outdated versions of software.

- **Common Vulnerabilities**:
  - **Directory Traversal**: If Apache is misconfigured, attackers can manipulate file paths to access files outside of the web root directory, potentially exposing sensitive files on the server.

- **Denial of Service (DoS)**: Apache servers are often vulnerable to DoS attacks, where excessive resource usage (such as memory or CPU) can cause the server to crash or become unresponsive.
- **Insecure Configuration**: By default, Apache has configurations that may be insecure, such as leaving unnecessary modules enabled, exposing server details, or allowing overly permissive file permissions.
- **CVE-2017-15715**: A critical vulnerability in Apache that allowed remote attackers to cause a segmentation fault (crash) and potentially execute arbitrary code by sending a specially crafted HTTP request.

- **Mitigation**:
  - Regularly update Apache and its components to the latest versions.
  - Disable unnecessary modules and services to reduce the attack surface.
  - Configure proper access controls and permissions for files and directories.
  - Implement Web Application Firewalls (WAF) and intrusion detection systems (IDS) to monitor for suspicious traffic.

2. IIS Web Server Vulnerabilities

Internet Information Services (IIS) is a proprietary web server from Microsoft that is commonly used in Windows environments. Like Apache, IIS is a frequent target for attackers, especially in environments where it is not securely configured or patched. IIS vulnerabilities are often linked to improper configuration or poorly managed web applications.

- **Common Vulnerabilities**:
    - **Default Configurations**: IIS often ships with default settings that are insecure, such as directory listings or sample web pages that may give attackers useful information about the server's environment.
    - **Buffer Overflow Vulnerabilities**: IIS has been susceptible to buffer overflow attacks, where an attacker exploits vulnerabilities in the server software to execute arbitrary code.
    - **Remote Code Execution (RCE)**: Older versions of IIS have had vulnerabilities (such as the one in **CVE-2000-0010**) that allowed attackers to execute remote code through misconfigured CGI scripts or malformed requests.
    - **File and Directory Disclosure**: Misconfigurations in IIS can allow attackers to enumerate directories or retrieve sensitive information from the file system.

- **Mitigation**:
  - Regularly patch IIS to address any known vulnerabilities.
  - Disable or remove unnecessary features, such as the WebDAV service, if not needed.
  - Limit access to sensitive directories and files using proper access control lists (ACLs) and permissions.
  - Employ **Security-Enhanced Windows** settings and use IIS logging to monitor and alert on suspicious activity.

Techniques for Exploiting Server Weaknesses

Exploiting web server vulnerabilities allows attackers to gain unauthorized access to sensitive data or take control of the web server. Ethical hackers use several techniques to exploit server weaknesses during penetration testing. Here are some of the most commonly used methods:

1. Remote Code Execution (RCE)

Remote code execution (RCE) occurs when an attacker is able to run arbitrary code on a server. This is often possible through vulnerabilities in server software (e.g., buffer overflows, improper input validation, or insecure configurations).

- **How it Works**: Attackers may exploit RCE vulnerabilities by sending a malicious payload that executes on the server, providing the attacker with full control over the server.

- **Example**: A vulnerability in an Apache module could allow an attacker to upload a malicious PHP file that, once executed, gives the attacker access to the server.

- **Mitigation**: Secure the web server by disabling or restricting file uploads, ensuring that user inputs are sanitized, and keeping the server software up-to-date. Implementing proper access control policies and securing the server's configuration files also helps mitigate RCE attacks.

2. Directory Traversal

Directory traversal (also known as path traversal) is a vulnerability that occurs when a web server improperly sanitizes user input, allowing an attacker to access directories outside of the web root. This can expose sensitive files, such as configuration files, source code, or logs.

- **How it Works**: In a directory traversal attack, an attacker crafts a request with directory traversal characters (e.g., ../) that trick the server into revealing files from outside the web root directory.

- **Example**: A web server might allow users to specify a file path via a URL parameter. If the server fails to properly sanitize the input, an attacker could manipulate the parameter to access files like /etc/passwd or C:\Windows\System32\config.

- **Mitigation**: Ensure that input validation is performed on all user-supplied data, especially file paths. Use secure coding practices to limit user access to specific directories and prevent directory traversal.

3. Cross-Site Scripting (XSS)

Cross-site scripting (XSS) is a vulnerability that occurs when a web server allows malicious scripts to be injected into web pages. When executed in the victim's browser, the malicious code can steal sensitive information, perform actions on behalf of the user, or deface the website.

- **How it Works**: An attacker injects malicious JavaScript into user input fields (such as comment sections, search boxes, or forms), which is then reflected in the server's response. When a legitimate user visits the page, the script executes in their browser.

- **Example**: An attacker could inject a script that steals a user's session cookies, allowing them to hijack the user's session.

- **Mitigation**: Implement proper input validation and output encoding to prevent the execution of malicious scripts. Use Content Security Policy (CSP) headers to restrict the sources from which scripts can be loaded.

4. Denial of Service (DoS) and Distributed Denial of Service (DDoS)

A **Denial of Service (DoS)** attack aims to overwhelm a web server by flooding it with excessive requests, making it unavailable to legitimate users. A **Distributed Denial of Service (DDoS)** attack is a more powerful form of DoS, where the attack is distributed across multiple machines, often using a botnet to generate massive traffic.

- **How it Works**: Attackers can flood a web server with requests, either by exploiting vulnerabilities in the server's software or by overwhelming the server with traffic. The goal is to exhaust system resources (CPU, memory, bandwidth) and disrupt service.

- **Example**: A DDoS attack on a popular website could involve sending millions of HTTP requests per second, rendering the server slow or completely unresponsive.

- **Mitigation**: Protect the server with **rate limiting**, **traffic filtering**, and **load balancing** to distribute traffic across multiple servers. Implementing Web Application Firewalls (WAFs) and using DDoS mitigation services can help absorb malicious traffic.

Steps to Secure Web Servers from Attacks

Securing web servers is a multifaceted process that involves proper configuration, regular updates, and proactive monitoring. Below are the key steps to take in securing Apache, IIS, or any other web server against common vulnerabilities and exploits:

1. Keep Software Updated

Regularly update the web server software and associated applications (such as CMS, databases, and plugins) to patch known vulnerabilities. Many exploits are successful simply because the server is running outdated or unpatched software.

- **How to Mitigate**: Subscribe to security mailing lists for your web server software to receive alerts about new vulnerabilities and patches. Implement a routine for applying patches and updates as soon as they are available.

2. Disable Unnecessary Services and Modules

Many web servers come with services and modules that are enabled by default but are not necessary for your environment. Leaving these services enabled can increase the attack surface of your server.

- **How to Mitigate**: Disable any unnecessary modules (e.g., WebDAV, FTP) and services (e.g., SSL/TLS if not required) in the web server configuration files. Perform a service audit to identify and disable any unused services.

3. Harden Server Configurations

A well-hardened server configuration can significantly reduce the likelihood of an attack. This includes setting up proper file permissions, disabling directory listing, and securing sensitive configuration files.

- **How to Mitigate**: Implement **secure HTTP headers** such as **Strict-Transport-Security (HSTS)**, **X-Content-Type-Options**, and **X-Frame-Options** to improve the security of the web server. Ensure that configuration files (e.g., httpd.conf, web.config) are not publicly accessible and are adequately protected.

4. Use Strong Authentication and Access Controls

Implement strong authentication methods (e.g., multi-factor authentication) and enforce strict access control measures for administrative users.

- **How to Mitigate**: Use **role-based access control (RBAC)** to ensure that users and administrators only have the necessary privileges. Regularly audit user accounts and permissions to ensure compliance with the principle of least privilege.

5. Encrypt Communications

Ensure that all sensitive data transmitted between clients and the web server is encrypted using secure protocols like **HTTPS** with

TLS. This prevents attackers from intercepting data during transmission.

- **How to Mitigate**: Obtain and install valid SSL/TLS certificates from trusted Certificate Authorities (CAs). Configure your web server to enforce the use of HTTPS and disable outdated or insecure protocols (e.g., SSLv2, SSLv3, and early versions of TLS).

6. Monitor and Log Activities

Enable detailed logging on your web server and continuously monitor for suspicious activity. Logs can help detect malicious behavior early and serve as valuable evidence during an investigation.

- **How to Mitigate**: Configure logging for all server actions, including access logs, error logs, and authentication attempts. Use **Security Information and Event Management (SIEM)** tools to analyze logs and alert administrators to suspicious activity in real-time.

Web servers are often a primary target for attackers due to their accessibility and the sensitive information they process. Exploiting vulnerabilities in web servers such as Apache and IIS can lead to significant security breaches, including data theft, denial of service, and remote code execution. By understanding common server vulnerabilities and using effective penetration testing techniques, ethical hackers can identify weaknesses before they are exploited by malicious actors.

Securing web servers requires a combination of strategies, including applying patches, disabling unnecessary services, hardening server configurations, enforcing strong authentication practices, encrypting data, and continuous monitoring. By following these steps, organizations can significantly reduce the risk of web server attacks and better protect their sensitive data and infrastructure from compromise.

Chapter 15: Post-Exploitation and Maintaining Access

What Happens After an Exploit is Successful?

After an exploit is successful, the ethical hacker (or attacker) gains unauthorized access to the target system. However, the immediate goal of exploitation is not merely to gain access; it is to further assess the system, gather valuable information, and ultimately determine how much damage could be done, or what sensitive data can be stolen or modified. The post-exploitation phase is crucial for determining the level of access and the potential consequences of a successful exploit.

The post-exploitation phase involves:

1. Assessing the Compromised System

Once an attacker has exploited a vulnerability and gained access to the system, they need to assess the environment and gather information to determine the next steps. This involves:

- **Identifying the target system's configuration**: The attacker will gather details such as the operating system, installed software, users and groups, file system layout, network configurations, and any connected devices or systems.

- **Examining security measures**: Attackers look for existing security controls, such as firewalls, intrusion detection systems (IDS), and antivirus software, which may alert administrators to the breach.
- **Identifying critical assets**: The attacker will try to identify valuable data, such as financial records, intellectual property, or sensitive client information, which could be the focus of the attack.

2. Clearing Logs and Hiding Evidence

In real-world attacks, attackers often try to cover their tracks to avoid detection. This is especially true when the attacker is working under the assumption that the victim might notice their activities and respond. This involves clearing logs, hiding files, and erasing traces that can lead back to the initial exploit.

- **Deleting or modifying log entries**: Attackers often manipulate or delete system logs to erase any evidence of their activities, such as unauthorized access attempts or exploit use.
- **Hiding malicious files**: Malicious scripts or tools used to maintain access can be hidden in system files or directories that are less likely to be examined by administrators.

3. Escalating Privileges

Once access is gained, the next step is often to escalate privileges in order to gain more control over the system. Privilege escalation is the process of elevating the current user's permissions to gain administrative or root access, which provides full control over the system.

Maintaining Access and Privilege Escalation Techniques

After gaining access, attackers or ethical hackers use various techniques to maintain control over the system. Privilege escalation ensures that the attacker can retain control even if the initial access vector is patched or closed.

1. Maintaining Access

Maintaining access is essential for attackers, especially when they intend to return to the compromised system later. This is usually done by installing backdoors or creating new accounts with elevated privileges. Several techniques are used to maintain access:

- **Creating backdoors**: A backdoor allows attackers to access the system at a later time without being detected. This could involve installing a remote access tool (RAT) such as **Netcat** or **Metasploit** to maintain access even after the initial exploit is patched.
- **Creating new user accounts**: Attackers may create new user accounts with administrative or root privileges to ensure they can return to the system at any time. These accounts

may be hidden by configuring them to not show up in system user lists.

- **Installing persistence mechanisms**: Techniques like setting up scheduled tasks or adding malicious entries to startup files can make sure that the attacker's access remains active even after system reboots.

2. Privilege Escalation Techniques

Once initial access is gained, attackers typically attempt to escalate their privileges to gain full administrative or root access. This is necessary to bypass access control restrictions and gain full control over the target system. There are several techniques for privilege escalation:

- **Exploiting vulnerabilities in the system**: Many systems have unpatched vulnerabilities that can be exploited to escalate privileges. For example, exploiting a **buffer overflow vulnerability** in a kernel module might give the attacker root access.
- **Misconfigured permissions**: Sometimes, poor configurations or overly permissive file permissions can allow attackers to escalate their privileges. For instance, a non-privileged user might be able to write to a file or execute a script that was intended to be restricted to an admin user.
- **Abusing setuid/setgid programs**: On Linux-based systems, files with the **setuid** or **setgid** bit set allow users to execute

programs with the privileges of the file's owner or group. Attackers can exploit these programs if they are insecurely configured, allowing them to escalate their privileges.

- **Credential harvesting**: Attackers can gather user credentials, often through **keylogging** or **sniffing network traffic**, and use these credentials to access higher-privileged accounts.

- **Password cracking**: If attackers gain access to password hashes, they may use brute-force or dictionary attacks to crack weak passwords and gain administrative access.

3. Using Metasploit for Post-Exploitation

After a successful exploitation, tools like **Metasploit** play a significant role in maintaining access and escalating privileges. Metasploit provides various post-exploitation modules that allow attackers to interact with the compromised system, gather information, and maintain access.

- **Key Post-Exploitation Features**:
  - **Meterpreter**: A powerful Metasploit payload that enables attackers to maintain access, move laterally within the network, and even capture screenshots, webcam feeds, and keystrokes from the target system.
  - **Privilege Escalation**: Metasploit has modules designed to exploit known vulnerabilities and

escalate privileges, such as **Linux Kernel Exploit** and **Windows Exploit Suggester**.

o **Pivoting**: Attackers can use the compromised system as a stepping stone to move laterally within the network to other systems, using techniques like tunneling and proxying.

Real-World Example of a Post-Exploitation Scenario

The 2017 WannaCry Ransomware Attack

One of the most significant post-exploitation scenarios in recent years was the **WannaCry ransomware attack** that hit thousands of organizations globally in May 2017. WannaCry exploited a vulnerability in Windows SMB (Server Message Block) protocol, which was publicly disclosed by the Shadow Brokers hacker group. The vulnerability was dubbed **EternalBlue**, and it allowed attackers to propagate the ransomware rapidly across networks.

How Post-Exploitation Was Achieved:

1. **Initial Access**: The initial attack vector was the exploitation of the SMB vulnerability, which allowed attackers to gain initial access to unpatched Windows systems. Once inside, attackers leveraged **EternalBlue** to move laterally across networks.

2. **Privilege Escalation**: In many cases, the attackers used **Metasploit** to exploit further vulnerabilities and escalate their privileges, taking full control of vulnerable systems. This enabled them to deploy the ransomware payload and spread it to other machines on the same network.

3. **Maintaining Access**: Once the ransomware was deployed, attackers ensured that they could continue to access compromised systems. They often installed backdoors or used other persistence techniques, such as **WMI** (Windows Management Instrumentation) to reinfect the system after reboots.

4. **Ransomware Deployment**: The payload encrypted critical files and demanded payment in cryptocurrency (Bitcoin) in exchange for the decryption key. The attack affected over 200,000 computers in 150 countries.

Mitigation Lessons:

- **Patching and Updates**: The attack exploited a vulnerability in unpatched Windows systems. This highlights the importance of timely patching and maintaining up-to-date systems.

- **Network Segmentation**: Proper network segmentation would have limited the lateral movement of the attack, preventing it from affecting large swathes of the organization.

- **Use of Antivirus and Endpoint Detection**: Many organizations did not have sufficient endpoint detection or antivirus solutions to catch the ransomware in its early stages.

Post-exploitation is a critical phase of any penetration test, as it involves maintaining access to the compromised system and escalating privileges to gain full control. Successful exploitation is only the beginning; attackers seek to move laterally, gather sensitive data, and ensure they can persist within the target network. Privilege escalation techniques, such as exploiting unpatched vulnerabilities or misconfigured permissions, are key methods for gaining deeper access.

By understanding the techniques and tools used during post-exploitation, such as **Metasploit, Meterpreter**, and various privilege escalation methods, ethical hackers can help organizations identify vulnerabilities before they are exploited by malicious actors. Proper mitigation, including patching, strong authentication, and regular monitoring, is essential to securing systems and preventing attackers from gaining or maintaining access.

Chapter 16: Ethical Hacking in Cloud Environments

The Rise of Cloud Computing and Its Security Challenges

Cloud computing has transformed the way organizations deploy, manage, and scale their IT infrastructure. With cloud platforms like **Amazon Web Services (AWS)**, **Microsoft Azure**, and **Google Cloud Platform (GCP)**, businesses can rent computing resources (such as storage, processing power, and networking) on-demand, without needing to maintain their own physical infrastructure. This flexibility, scalability, and cost-efficiency have made cloud computing an attractive option for organizations across industries.

However, the rise of cloud computing has also introduced new security challenges that organizations must address to protect their data, applications, and services. While cloud providers typically offer robust security features, the responsibility for securing the cloud environment is shared between the cloud provider and the customer. This shared responsibility model means that while providers secure the infrastructure, customers are responsible for securing their data, applications, and user access.

Key Cloud Security Challenges:

1. **Data Breaches**: Cloud environments store vast amounts of sensitive data, making them prime targets for attackers. Poor access controls, misconfigurations, or vulnerabilities in cloud services can expose data to unauthorized access.

2. **Misconfigurations**: Misconfigured cloud resources are one of the most common causes of security incidents. Whether it's improperly configured storage buckets, overly permissive access permissions, or exposing sensitive data in public environments, misconfigurations are a frequent point of weakness.

3. **Lack of Visibility and Control**: Cloud environments are often distributed, with resources located across different data centers, regions, or even multiple cloud providers. This can make it difficult for organizations to maintain visibility and control over their infrastructure, leading to gaps in security monitoring.

4. **Identity and Access Management (IAM)**: Cloud services provide extensive access controls, but if IAM policies are not properly configured, attackers can exploit weak authentication or unauthorized access to escalate privileges and compromise systems.

5. **Shared Responsibility**: As mentioned, the shared responsibility model can create confusion. Organizations may assume the cloud provider handles all aspects of

security, when, in reality, they must secure their data and applications on top of the cloud provider's infrastructure.

Penetration Testing in Cloud Environments (AWS, Azure, GCP)

Penetration testing in cloud environments requires a different approach compared to traditional on-premises testing. While cloud providers offer extensive security features, ethical hackers must understand the shared responsibility model and navigate the provider's guidelines and constraints on penetration testing.

1. Penetration Testing in AWS (Amazon Web Services)

AWS provides a comprehensive suite of services, but it also has specific rules and guidelines for penetration testing. AWS customers are generally permitted to perform penetration testing on their own instances and services, but there are some restrictions and rules to follow:

- **What's Allowed**:
    - Testing can be conducted on the instances you own, including EC2 instances, RDS databases, and S3 buckets (with proper permissions).
    - AWS allows penetration testing of web applications hosted on AWS, provided no attacks are directed at the underlying infrastructure.
- **What's Not Allowed**:

- o **AWS-managed services**, such as AWS Lambda, Route 53, or CloudFront, cannot be subjected to penetration testing without prior approval.
- o Attacks on the infrastructure, such as attempting to exploit vulnerabilities in AWS's core services, are prohibited.

- **Common Testing Areas in AWS**:
  - o **Access Control and IAM Policies**: Testing for weak permissions, excessive access rights, and misconfigured roles or policies.
  - o **Instance Security**: Testing EC2 instances for known vulnerabilities and configuration flaws.
  - o **Storage**: Scanning for misconfigured S3 buckets or databases that might expose sensitive data.
  - o **Networking**: Examining VPC configurations, security groups, and firewalls to ensure proper segmentation and protection against external threats.

2. Penetration Testing in Azure

Microsoft Azure also has guidelines for penetration testing within its platform. While it provides customers with extensive tools for securing their environments, ethical hackers must adhere to its specific rules for testing.

- **What's Allowed**:

- o Customers can perform penetration testing on their own virtual machines, web apps, and storage resources.
- o Azure's **Network Security Groups (NSGs)**, **Key Vaults**, and **App Services** can be tested for weaknesses.
- **What's Not Allowed**:
  - o Testing Azure's infrastructure, such as the core network or components like Azure AD, requires prior approval.
  - o Any denial-of-service (DoS) or Distributed Denial of Service (DDoS) testing is prohibited.
- **Common Testing Areas in Azure**:
  - o **Identity Management**: Assessing Azure AD and examining IAM policies, permissions, and user roles for potential misconfigurations.
  - o **Virtual Machines**: Checking for unpatched vulnerabilities in VMs and ensuring proper segmentation and isolation.
  - o **Storage**: Ensuring proper encryption and access control for blob storage, databases, and file shares.
  - o **Web Applications**: Testing for vulnerabilities such as SQL injection, XSS, and misconfigured Azure App Services.

3. Penetration Testing in GCP (Google Cloud Platform)

GCP also provides penetration testing guidelines, and ethical hackers must ensure they adhere to GCP's testing policies to avoid any unintended violations. GCP has a more permissive policy compared to other cloud providers, allowing a wider range of testing activities.

- **What's Allowed**:
  - Customers can perform penetration testing on most Google Cloud services, including Compute Engine instances, Cloud Storage, and Kubernetes Engine.
  - Testing is permitted for applications, virtual machines, containers, and cloud services managed by the customer.
- **What's Not Allowed**:
  - Similar to other cloud platforms, GCP prohibits penetration testing of its infrastructure, including testing the network layer or GCP-managed services like Cloud Load Balancer, Cloud DNS, and Cloud Identity.
  - Attacks aimed at Google's production systems or services are forbidden.
- **Common Testing Areas in GCP**:
  - **IAM Configuration**: Testing for overly permissive IAM roles and the potential for privilege escalation.

- o **Compute Engine**: Exploiting weaknesses in VM configurations and patching, testing for weak access controls on the VMs.

- o **Networking**: Examining firewall rules, VPC configurations, and subnets for potential vulnerabilities or misconfigurations that could lead to unauthorized access.

- o **Cloud Storage**: Ensuring Cloud Storage buckets are properly secured and not publicly accessible.

Case Study of a Cloud Environment Security Breach

The Capital One Data Breach (2019)

One of the most significant cloud security breaches occurred in 2019, when **Capital One**, a major financial institution, experienced a massive data breach involving **Amazon Web Services (AWS)**. The breach affected over 100 million customers and exposed sensitive data, including names, addresses, credit scores, and social security numbers.

How the Attack Happened:

- The attacker exploited a **misconfigured AWS WAF (Web Application Firewall)** in the Capital One cloud environment. The attacker used a vulnerability in the configuration of a **metadata service** on an AWS EC2 instance.

- The vulnerability allowed the attacker to run unauthorized commands, leading to the compromise of sensitive data stored in S3 buckets.
- The breach was due to an overly permissive configuration in AWS that allowed the attacker to gain access to Capital One's data without triggering alerts.

Post-Breach Investigation:

- The attack was discovered after the attacker attempted to steal data and upload it to an external server. The attacker was quickly apprehended, and the breach was publicly disclosed.
- The breach raised awareness about the risks of **misconfigured cloud services** and **inadequate access controls**. Although AWS's infrastructure was secure, Capital One failed to properly secure their cloud configuration and sensitive data.
- The incident led to a **$80 million fine** for Capital One and highlighted the importance of securing cloud resources, implementing least privilege access, and monitoring cloud configurations regularly.

Mitigation Lessons:

- **Secure Configuration**: Ensure that all cloud resources, including firewalls, storage buckets, and application services, are configured securely.

- **Access Control**: Implement the principle of least privilege in IAM policies to restrict access to sensitive data.

- **Regular Auditing**: Regularly audit cloud resources and configurations to identify potential vulnerabilities before they can be exploited.

- **Monitoring and Alerts**: Implement strong monitoring and alerting mechanisms to detect unauthorized activity and ensure prompt response to potential incidents.

As cloud computing continues to grow in popularity, ethical hackers must be equipped to test the security of cloud environments such as AWS, Azure, and GCP. Each cloud provider offers different configurations, tools, and rules for penetration testing, but the core principles remain the same: securing data, maintaining access controls, and ensuring proper configurations.

Penetration testing in the cloud focuses on assessing vulnerabilities such as misconfigured services, weak IAM policies, insecure data storage, and network vulnerabilities. The **Capital One breach** serves as a stark reminder of the importance of securing cloud environments, as even a single misconfiguration can lead to devastating consequences. By understanding cloud security challenges and best practices, organizations can better protect their cloud resources and reduce the risk of data breaches and other security incidents.

Chapter 17: Penetration Testing for Mobile Applications

Security Risks in Mobile Apps

Mobile applications have become an integral part of daily life, with millions of apps available across platforms like **iOS** and **Android**. Mobile apps are used for a wide range of activities, from social media and online shopping to banking and healthcare. However, the rapid growth of the mobile app industry has introduced new security challenges and risks.

Some of the most common security risks associated with mobile apps include:

1. Insecure Data Storage

Mobile devices often store sensitive information, such as user credentials, personal data, and financial details. Insecure data storage occurs when sensitive information is stored in an unencrypted or poorly encrypted form, making it vulnerable to extraction by attackers.

- **Example**: Sensitive information like passwords or authentication tokens may be stored in plaintext in app data or local storage, which could be easily accessed if the device is compromised or rooted.

2. Insecure Communication

Mobile apps frequently transmit sensitive data over the network. If the data is not properly encrypted during transmission, it can be intercepted by attackers using methods like **man-in-the-middle (MITM)** attacks.

- **Example**: If an app sends unencrypted data over HTTP instead of HTTPS, an attacker could intercept sensitive information like credit card details, usernames, or passwords.

3. Improper Implementation of Authentication and Session Management

Authentication and session management are critical for mobile apps, but many apps fail to implement secure practices. This can result in weak password policies, insecure session handling, and the ability for attackers to hijack user sessions.

- **Example**: An attacker may exploit weak session management (e.g., session IDs not being securely stored or transmitted) to impersonate a legitimate user.

4. Reverse Engineering and Code Decompilation

Mobile apps, especially those built for **Android**, are susceptible to reverse engineering. Attackers can decompile the APK (Android application package) or binary to view the source code and potentially discover vulnerabilities, hardcoded secrets, or sensitive information.

- **Example**: If API keys, passwords, or other sensitive data are hardcoded within the app's code, attackers can extract them by reverse engineering the app.

5. Insecure APIs

Mobile apps rely heavily on APIs (Application Programming Interfaces) to communicate with back-end servers. If the APIs are insecure or poorly configured, attackers may be able to exploit vulnerabilities in the API to gain unauthorized access to data or systems.

- **Example**: An app may fail to properly authenticate API requests or might expose too much information via APIs, allowing attackers to access sensitive user data or manipulate application behavior.

6. Insufficient App Permissions

Mobile apps can request various permissions from users, such as access to the camera, microphone, contacts, and location. In some cases, apps request unnecessary permissions or misuse the permissions they have been granted.

- **Example**: A seemingly harmless app may request access to the device's camera or microphone without a legitimate reason, potentially compromising user privacy.

7. Security Flaws in Third-Party Libraries

Mobile apps often integrate third-party libraries or SDKs (Software Development Kits) to implement features like social media login, payments, or analytics. These libraries may contain vulnerabilities that can be exploited if not regularly updated.

- **Example**: An app using an outdated third-party library with a known vulnerability may be exposed to attacks, even if the app itself is secure.

Techniques and Tools for Testing Mobile Apps

Penetration testing for mobile applications requires specialized tools and techniques due to the unique characteristics of mobile devices and apps. Testing involves assessing both the mobile app itself and the backend systems it communicates with.

1. Mobile App Reverse Engineering

Reverse engineering involves decompiling or disassembling the mobile app's code to analyze it for vulnerabilities, hardcoded secrets, or insecure practices.

- **Tools**:

o **JADX**: A decompiler that converts Android APK files into Java source code, making it easier to analyze the app's logic.

o **APKTool**: A tool for decompiling Android APKs, allowing testers to modify resources and inspect AndroidManifest.xml and other app components.

o **Frida**: A dynamic instrumentation toolkit that allows ethical hackers to hook into a mobile app and modify its runtime behavior to test for vulnerabilities in real-time.

2. Static and Dynamic Analysis

- **Static Analysis**: This involves analyzing the app's code without executing it. Tools for static analysis help identify coding flaws, hardcoded secrets, and other vulnerabilities.

  o **Tools**:

    ▪ **MobSF (Mobile Security Framework)**: An automated static and dynamic analysis tool for iOS and Android apps. It provides detailed reports on security vulnerabilities.

    ▪ **Checkmarx**: A static code analysis tool that scans the source code or binaries for vulnerabilities and security flaws.

- **Dynamic Analysis**: This involves running the app in a controlled environment to monitor its behavior and interactions with the device. Dynamic analysis helps identify issues that arise only during execution, such as improper session handling, API vulnerabilities, and insecure data transmission.

- o **Tools**:
  - **Burp Suite**: Used to intercept and analyze HTTP/HTTPS traffic between the mobile app and the backend server to identify security flaws in the API communication.
  - **OWASP ZAP**: Another tool for intercepting and analyzing traffic and scanning mobile apps for vulnerabilities.

3. API Testing

Mobile apps often rely on APIs to communicate with backend servers. Testing these APIs for vulnerabilities, such as improper authentication, authorization flaws, or excessive data exposure, is crucial.

- **Tools**:
  - o **Postman**: A popular API testing tool that allows testers to send custom API requests and analyze responses.
  - o **OWASP Amass**: A tool for uncovering hidden APIs or endpoints, helping testers find less obvious attack vectors.

4. Network Traffic Analysis

To test for insecure communication, penetration testers can intercept and analyze the network traffic between the mobile app and the backend server.

- **Tools**:
    - o **Wireshark**: A network protocol analyzer that can capture and analyze packets to look for sensitive data that is transmitted insecurely (e.g., unencrypted passwords).
    - o **SSLStrip**: A tool used to intercept and downgrade HTTPS connections to HTTP, allowing testers to capture traffic that would otherwise be encrypted.

5. Testing App Permissions

Ethical hackers should test if the app requests unnecessary permissions and whether it uses those permissions in a secure manner.

- **Tools**:
    - o **APKTool**: Used to inspect and modify the Android app to check how it handles permissions.
    - o **Xposed Framework**: A framework for Android that allows testers to change the behavior of apps at runtime, which can help analyze how apps request and use permissions.

6. Automated Mobile App Security Scanning

For comprehensive testing, automated mobile app security scanners can help identify a wide range of vulnerabilities across different platforms.

- **Tools**:
    - **MobSF**: Offers both static and dynamic analysis, with support for Android, iOS, and hybrid apps.
    - **AppScan**: A security testing tool that can analyze mobile apps for vulnerabilities in code and functionality.

Real-World Mobile App Penetration Testing Case Study

The Instagram Mobile App Data Breach (2019)

In 2019, **Instagram**, one of the most popular social media platforms, experienced a security breach due to a vulnerability in its mobile app. The breach involved an insecure API that allowed an attacker to access private information of millions of Instagram users.

The Attack:

- The breach occurred due to an insecure API used for retrieving users' phone numbers and email addresses. Attackers exploited the flaw by sending requests to the API, using user IDs and obtaining phone numbers and email addresses linked to users' accounts.

- Although the app itself was not directly compromised, the vulnerability in the backend API exposed sensitive user information without the users' knowledge.

The Response:

- Instagram quickly patched the API vulnerability, but the incident raised awareness about the need to secure backend systems, particularly APIs that interact with mobile apps. In this case, the lack of proper authentication and authorization checks allowed unauthorized access to private data.

Lessons Learned:

1. **Secure API Endpoints**: Mobile app developers should ensure that APIs are properly secured with strong authentication and authorization mechanisms. All API endpoints should validate user identity and ensure that users only have access to their own data.
2. **Encryption**: Ensure that sensitive data, such as personal information and login credentials, is encrypted both at rest and in transit.
3. **Input Validation**: Proper input validation and parameter checks can prevent attackers from abusing API endpoints and accessing unauthorized data.

4. **Vulnerability Scanning and Penetration Testing**: Regular security assessments, including penetration testing and vulnerability scanning of mobile apps and their backend APIs, are essential for identifying weaknesses before they are exploited.

Mobile applications are an integral part of modern digital services, but they are also prime targets for attackers seeking to exploit vulnerabilities. Penetration testing for mobile apps involves a combination of static and dynamic analysis, reverse engineering, and testing the app's communication channels, APIs, and backend systems. Tools like **Burp Suite**, **MobSF**, and **Wireshark** help ethical hackers identify vulnerabilities and weaknesses in mobile apps, ultimately providing actionable recommendations for improving app security.

The **Instagram breach** highlights the importance of securing both mobile apps and the APIs they interact with. By adopting best practices for mobile app development, such as securing APIs, encrypting sensitive data, and regularly testing the app for vulnerabilities, organizations can significantly reduce the risk of data breaches and ensure that their mobile applications remain secure.

Chapter 18: Internet of Things (IoT) Penetration Testing

The Vulnerabilities in IoT Devices

The **Internet of Things (IoT)** has dramatically transformed the way we interact with the world around us. From smart home devices, wearables, and healthcare equipment to industrial machines and connected vehicles, IoT devices are becoming an integral part of modern life. However, the proliferation of these connected devices has introduced significant security challenges. Many IoT devices lack proper security measures and can become entry points for cyberattacks.

The most common vulnerabilities in IoT devices include:

1. Weak Authentication and Access Control

Many IoT devices use default, weak passwords or no authentication at all, making them vulnerable to unauthorized access. Attackers can easily gain control of devices if they exploit these weak authentication mechanisms.

- **Example**: Many smart cameras and home automation devices come with default passwords, and users often neglect to change them, making it easier for attackers to compromise them.

2. Insecure Communication

IoT devices often transmit sensitive data over wireless networks, such as Wi-Fi, Bluetooth, or Zigbee. If the communication is not properly encrypted, attackers can intercept and manipulate the data, potentially gaining access to sensitive information.

- **Example**: Without end-to-end encryption, attackers can perform **Man-in-the-Middle (MITM)** attacks and eavesdrop on data being sent between devices or between devices and servers.

3. Lack of Regular Updates and Patching

Many IoT manufacturers fail to provide regular security updates or patches to fix known vulnerabilities. This leaves devices exposed to cybercriminals who can exploit these flaws.

- **Example**: IoT devices may run outdated versions of software or firmware, which may contain known vulnerabilities that have been exploited in other attacks.

4. Insecure APIs

IoT devices often interact with mobile applications or cloud-based platforms via APIs. If these APIs are insecure, they can expose sensitive data or provide a vector for attackers to exploit the device or the network.

- **Example**: Insecure APIs can allow attackers to access or modify the device's configuration or extract sensitive user data such as location information, voice recordings, or health metrics.

5. Inadequate Device and Network Segmentation

Many IoT devices are connected to home or corporate networks, but they often lack proper network segmentation. This means that if an attacker compromises one device, they could use it as a stepping stone to access other parts of the network.

- **Example**: If an attacker gains control of a smart thermostat, they might use it as a gateway to compromise other connected devices like security cameras or home automation systems.

6. Physical Attacks

Some IoT devices are deployed in physical spaces and can be easily tampered with or attacked. Attackers with physical access to the devices can potentially bypass security controls or inject malicious software.

- **Example**: An attacker could gain physical access to an IoT device like a door lock or access control system, extract firmware, and manipulate the device to grant unauthorized access.

Techniques for IoT Penetration Testing

Penetration testing for IoT devices involves identifying vulnerabilities in the devices, their communication channels, and the infrastructure they are connected to. The goal of IoT penetration testing is to simulate real-world attacks to assess the security posture of IoT systems.

1. Device Discovery and Enumeration

The first step in IoT penetration testing is discovering and enumerating the devices present in the network. This helps ethical hackers identify the IoT devices and their associated vulnerabilities.

- **Techniques**:
  - **Network Scanning**: Tools like **Nmap** and **Wireshark** can be used to scan the network and identify connected devices, their IP addresses, and open ports.
  - **Service Fingerprinting**: Once devices are identified, penetration testers use service fingerprinting tools to gather detailed information about the services running on these devices.

2. Vulnerability Scanning

Once the devices and services are identified, the next step is to perform vulnerability scanning to detect known weaknesses.

- **Techniques**:
  - **Automated Vulnerability Scanning**: Tools like **Nessus**, **OpenVAS**, and **Shodan** can scan devices for vulnerabilities like open ports, outdated software, weak default credentials, and insecure communication.
  - **Manual Testing**: Since automated tools may miss some vulnerabilities, ethical hackers perform manual testing to identify security flaws such as improper API configurations, lack of encryption, or weak access control mechanisms.

3. Network Traffic Analysis

Many IoT devices communicate with servers or cloud platforms via the internet. By analyzing the network traffic, ethical hackers can identify unencrypted communications, insecure protocols, or data leaks.

- **Techniques**:
  - **MITM Attacks**: Tools like **Ettercap** or **Wireshark** can be used to intercept and manipulate traffic between IoT devices and their servers, allowing

attackers to examine sensitive data or inject malicious commands.

- o **Traffic Analysis**: Ethical hackers monitor network traffic for anomalies, such as plaintext data being sent over HTTP or weak encryption methods, which could expose sensitive data to attackers.

4. Firmware and Software Analysis

IoT devices often run embedded software or firmware, which can be analyzed for vulnerabilities. Testing the firmware can help identify hardcoded credentials, insecure code, or vulnerabilities in the device's software stack.

- **Techniques**:
  - o **Firmware Dumping**: Attackers extract firmware from the IoT device using tools like **binwalk** or **JTAG** interfaces. This allows ethical hackers to analyze the firmware for vulnerabilities, including hardcoded passwords or insecure API calls.
  - o **Decompiling**: Once firmware is dumped, decompiling tools can be used to analyze the code and look for weaknesses in the device's software.

5. Exploiting Vulnerabilities

Once vulnerabilities are identified, ethical hackers will attempt to exploit them to assess the potential damage an attacker could cause.

- **Techniques**:
  - **Exploiting Default Passwords**: Many IoT devices come with weak default credentials. Ethical hackers can attempt to exploit this weakness by using default password lists or brute-forcing login attempts to gain unauthorized access.
  - **Command Injection**: If the device accepts commands from the user, ethical hackers can test for command injection vulnerabilities, where malicious commands can be executed on the device or server.

6. Post-Exploitation

After a successful exploit, ethical hackers work to maintain access to the IoT device and escalate privileges if possible.

- **Techniques**:
  - **Persistence**: Ethical hackers may install a backdoor or make changes to the device's firmware or configuration to maintain access.
  - **Privilege Escalation**: By exploiting further vulnerabilities in the device's configuration or code, ethical hackers may escalate their privileges to gain full control over the IoT device.

Real-World IoT Security Breach: The Mirai Botnet (2016)

One of the most significant IoT security breaches in recent years was the **Mirai botnet** attack, which occurred in 2016. The Mirai botnet was a large-scale distributed denial-of-service (DDoS) attack that used compromised IoT devices to flood websites with traffic, rendering them unavailable to users.

How the Attack Happened:

- **Compromised Devices**: The Mirai malware primarily targeted IoT devices such as IP cameras, DVRs, and routers. Many of these devices had weak or default passwords, which made them easy targets for the attackers.
- **Botnet Formation**: Once the Mirai malware infected the IoT devices, it turned them into "zombie" machines that could be controlled remotely by the attackers. The botnet then launched a massive DDoS attack against **Dyn**, a major DNS provider, disrupting access to large websites like Twitter, Reddit, and Spotify.

Impact:

- The attack caused major disruptions to internet services for millions of users. The Mirai botnet's scale and effectiveness demonstrated how insecure IoT devices could be used to cause widespread damage.

Lessons Learned:

1. **Device Hardening**: Many of the devices used in the Mirai botnet had weak default credentials. Manufacturers and users must change default passwords and use strong, unique credentials.

2. **IoT Device Security**: IoT devices should have built-in security mechanisms, such as encryption, secure authentication, and proper update mechanisms.

3. **Network Segmentation**: IoT devices should be isolated from critical parts of the network to prevent an attacker from using a compromised IoT device to move laterally across the network.

IoT devices are increasingly integrated into our daily lives, but their security vulnerabilities present significant risks. Penetration testing for IoT devices is essential to uncover weaknesses that could be exploited by attackers. By using techniques such as reverse engineering, network traffic analysis, firmware analysis, and vulnerability scanning, ethical hackers can identify vulnerabilities in IoT devices and help organizations secure them.

The **Mirai botnet** attack serves as a stark reminder of the dangers posed by insecure IoT devices. By following best practices for securing IoT devices, such as changing default credentials, using strong encryption, and applying regular patches, organizations can reduce the risk of IoT-based attacks and ensure that their devices remain secure. Penetration testing plays a critical role in identifying these vulnerabilities and mitigating the risks associated with IoT devices.

Chapter 19: Ethical Hacking and Privacy Laws

Understanding Privacy Laws (GDPR, HIPAA, CCPA)

As the practice of ethical hacking continues to grow, the need to understand privacy laws and their implications on security assessments becomes increasingly important. Ethical hackers must navigate these laws to ensure their testing activities do not violate the legal rights of individuals or organizations. Privacy laws are designed to protect personal data, ensure transparency in how data is handled, and hold organizations accountable for breaches. Below are some of the most significant privacy laws that ethical hackers must understand.

1. General Data Protection Regulation (GDPR)

The **GDPR**, implemented in May 2018, is a regulation established by the European Union to protect the personal data and privacy of EU citizens. It has far-reaching implications for any organization that handles EU residents' data, regardless of where the organization is based. GDPR aims to give individuals more control over their personal data and ensure that companies handling that data are accountable for its protection.

- **Key Provisions**:

- o **Data Subject Rights**: GDPR grants individuals several rights, including the right to access, rectify, or delete personal data, and the right to object to or restrict processing.

- o **Data Processing Transparency**: Organizations must be transparent about how personal data is collected, processed, and used.

- o **Data Protection by Design and Default**: Organizations must ensure that data protection is built into their systems and processes from the outset.

- o **Data Breach Notification**: GDPR mandates that organizations report any data breaches within 72 hours.

- **Impact on Ethical Hacking**: Ethical hackers must be cautious when handling personal data during penetration testing. Any unauthorized access, collection, or processing of personal data could lead to significant legal repercussions under GDPR.

2. Health Insurance Portability and Accountability Act (HIPAA)

HIPAA is a U.S. law that governs the protection of health information, primarily focusing on healthcare providers, insurers, and clearinghouses. The law ensures that personal health information (PHI) is properly secured and protected from unauthorized access.

- **Key Provisions**:
  - ○ **Privacy Rule**: Protects individuals' health information by restricting access to and sharing of PHI without consent.
  - ○ **Security Rule**: Sets standards for protecting electronic PHI (ePHI) through safeguards like encryption, access controls, and regular audits.
  - ○ **Breach Notification Rule**: Requires covered entities to notify individuals if their PHI is accessed, acquired, or disclosed inappropriately.
- **Impact on Ethical Hacking**: Ethical hackers must be extremely careful when testing healthcare organizations or healthcare-related apps, as accessing PHI without consent can lead to severe penalties. Ethical hackers should be fully aware of the scope of the test and ensure that they do not access or store PHI.

3. California Consumer Privacy Act (CCPA)

The **CCPA** is a California state law aimed at enhancing privacy rights for residents of California. It grants California residents the right to access, delete, and opt out of the sale of their personal data.

- **Key Provisions**:
  - ○ **Right to Know**: Consumers have the right to request information about the personal data collected about them.

- o **Right to Delete**: Consumers have the right to request the deletion of their personal data.

- o **Right to Opt-Out**: Consumers can request that businesses stop selling their personal data.

- o **Non-Discrimination**: Businesses cannot discriminate against consumers for exercising their privacy rights under the CCPA.

- **Impact on Ethical Hacking**: When performing penetration tests involving consumer data, ethical hackers must ensure that they do not violate CCPA provisions. This means avoiding unauthorized access or sale of personal information, and ensuring that consumers' data privacy rights are respected.

The Legal Boundaries of Ethical Hacking

Ethical hacking, often referred to as penetration testing, is conducted to identify vulnerabilities in systems to improve security. However, penetration testers must operate within the boundaries of the law. Unauthorized hacking, even for ethical purposes, is illegal. Ethical hackers must gain explicit written consent before conducting penetration testing on any system, network, or application.

1. Consent and Authorization

Before conducting any penetration testing activities, ethical hackers must obtain **explicit written consent** from the organization that owns the systems being tested. This ensures that the activities fall within the boundaries of the law. The written consent should specify the scope, limits, and permissions for testing, including:

- **Which systems are to be tested** (e.g., web applications, network infrastructure, mobile apps).
- **What types of tests** will be conducted (e.g., vulnerability scanning, social engineering, code analysis).
- **Timeframe** for testing and any constraints (e.g., testing outside of business hours).
- **Clear permission** to attempt exploits or access data during the testing process.

Without proper authorization, even if the intent is to improve security, penetration testing can be considered illegal, and the hacker could face civil or criminal charges.

2. Scope of Testing

Ethical hackers must strictly adhere to the agreed-upon **scope** of testing. Performing activities outside the agreed-upon boundaries could lead to unintended consequences, such as system downtime, data loss, or breaches of privacy laws. For example:

- Testing one application but accessing another without authorization can violate data protection laws and cause reputational damage.

- Testing sensitive customer data without consent could breach privacy laws like GDPR or CCPA.

3. Avoiding Data Exposure

While conducting penetration tests, ethical hackers must be extremely careful not to expose, alter, or misuse any sensitive data. Data handling must comply with relevant data protection laws, such as GDPR, HIPAA, or CCPA, which impose strict guidelines for the storage, access, and processing of personal data.

- Any sensitive data discovered during penetration testing should be securely handled and never stored without permission. If data is inadvertently exposed during testing, ethical hackers must report the incident immediately.

4. Adhering to Local Laws

Penetration testers must also be aware of the **jurisdictional boundaries** and legal frameworks that govern their activities. Laws regarding hacking and data protection can vary widely by region, so penetration testers need to familiarize themselves with local, state, and international laws.

- **Cross-border testing** can present challenges, as testing systems that span different jurisdictions might subject ethical hackers to multiple sets of regulations. For example, testing a cloud service with servers in the EU and the US could involve compliance with both GDPR and CCPA.

How to Conduct Penetration Tests Without Violating Laws

Ethical hackers can conduct penetration tests without violating laws by following a set of best practices that prioritize legality, consent, and respect for privacy rights:

1. Obtain Written Authorization

Before starting any penetration test, always obtain **written permission** from the organization that owns the systems being tested. The authorization document should outline the scope, testing methodology, and any limitations to ensure that testing remains within legal boundaries.

2. Define a Clear Scope

A clear and detailed **scope of testing** is essential. This defines which systems, applications, and devices are in-scope for testing, and any limitations should be clearly stated. This ensures that penetration testers do not accidentally target systems they were not authorized to test, which could result in legal issues.

3. Ensure Compliance with Privacy Laws

Penetration testers must ensure that they comply with relevant **privacy laws** when handling personal or sensitive data. If personal data is encountered during the test, ethical hackers should not misuse or expose it. Any testing that involves **personal health data**, **financial information**, or **customer data** should follow the appropriate laws, such as GDPR, HIPAA, or CCPA.

- **Data Masking**: If personal data is required for testing purposes, ensure that the data is anonymized or masked to protect privacy.

4. Use Secure Channels for Communication

When performing penetration testing, ethical hackers should communicate findings and vulnerabilities securely. Any sensitive data related to the test (e.g., discovered vulnerabilities, PII, passwords) should be transmitted through encrypted communication channels and stored securely.

5. Report Findings in a Responsible Manner

After completing the penetration test, ethical hackers should provide a **detailed and responsible report** to the organization. The report should clearly outline the vulnerabilities found, the risks they pose, and actionable recommendations for remediation. The report should be **confidential** and should not be disclosed to unauthorized parties.

6. Stay Updated on Legal Changes

Ethical hackers must stay informed about the latest changes to privacy laws, cybersecurity regulations, and industry standards. As data protection laws evolve, such as with the introduction of **new privacy laws** (e.g., Brazil's **LGPD** or India's **Personal Data**

Protection Bill), penetration testers need to adapt their practices to remain compliant.

Ethical hacking plays a crucial role in identifying vulnerabilities and improving security for organizations. However, penetration testers must carefully navigate the legal and ethical landscape, especially regarding privacy laws such as **GDPR, HIPAA**, and **CCPA**. By obtaining proper consent, adhering to the defined scope of testing, and respecting privacy regulations, ethical hackers can conduct effective security assessments without violating the law.

Penetration testing must always be conducted with full authorization and in compliance with relevant legal frameworks. This ensures that the testing is ethical, responsible, and beneficial to the organization, while safeguarding privacy rights and avoiding legal consequences. Ethical hackers who stay informed about privacy laws and best practices can provide valuable security services without crossing legal boundaries.

Chapter 20: Writing a Penetration Testing Report

Structure of a Penetration Testing Report

A **penetration testing report** is the primary deliverable that a penetration tester provides to a client after completing an engagement. It serves as both a documentation of the findings and a roadmap for remediation. A well-written report should be clear, concise, and tailored to the target audience, whether that be technical experts, IT administrators, or non-technical stakeholders such as management.

The structure of the report typically follows a logical flow, starting with an executive summary and then diving into the details of the findings, vulnerabilities, and recommendations. Here is a common structure for a penetration testing report:

1. Cover Page

The cover page should include basic information about the engagement, such as:

- The **title** of the report (e.g., "Penetration Test Report: Web Application Testing").
- The **client's name** and **organization**.
- The **date** the report was delivered.

- The **pen tester's contact information** or company details.
- **Confidentiality notice** (e.g., "This report is confidential and intended for the internal use of [Client's Organization Name].").

2. Table of Contents

A table of contents is important for navigating through the report, especially when it is lengthy. It should list major sections such as the executive summary, detailed findings, recommendations, and appendices.

3. Executive Summary

The executive summary provides a high-level overview of the penetration testing engagement, aimed at a non-technical audience (e.g., managers, executives). This section should be concise but informative, covering:

- **Objectives**: A brief description of the goals of the penetration test (e.g., testing the security of the network infrastructure or identifying vulnerabilities in a web application).
- **Scope**: A summary of what was tested, including which systems, networks, or applications were in-scope and out-of-scope.
- **Summary of Findings**: A high-level overview of the most critical vulnerabilities discovered during the testing, along

with their potential impact on the organization's security posture.

- **Recommendations**: A general statement of the recommended next steps for the organization to address the identified vulnerabilities.

4. Methodology

In this section, the penetration tester outlines the **testing methodology** used during the engagement. This helps the client understand the approach taken and the depth of the test. It includes:

- The **phases of testing** (e.g., information gathering, scanning, exploitation, post-exploitation).
- The **tools** and **techniques** used during the test (e.g., Nmap, Burp Suite, Metasploit, manual testing).
- A brief description of any **limitations** or **restrictions** during the test (e.g., testing was only performed during business hours, or certain systems were excluded from testing).

5. Findings

The findings section is the heart of the report and provides a detailed breakdown of all vulnerabilities discovered during the engagement. Each finding should include the following components:

- **Vulnerability Title**: A concise title summarizing the vulnerability (e.g., "SQL Injection in User Login Form").

- **Description**: A detailed explanation of the vulnerability, including how it was discovered, its potential impact, and why it is a risk to the organization.

- **Risk Rating**: A severity rating of the vulnerability, such as **Critical**, **High**, **Medium**, or **Low**, based on the potential damage it could cause (e.g., data theft, system compromise). Many organizations use the **CVSS** (Common Vulnerability Scoring System) for standardized risk ratings.

- **Evidence**: This may include screenshots, logs, or other proof that the vulnerability exists and was successfully exploited.

- **Remediation Advice**: High-level recommendations for fixing or mitigating the vulnerability.

6. Recommendations

This section provides actionable recommendations for each of the findings. The recommendations should be clear and practical, helping the client understand how to resolve or mitigate the vulnerabilities identified during the testing.

- **Prioritized Action Plan**: The report should help the client prioritize remediation efforts by focusing on high-risk vulnerabilities first, then medium and low-risk vulnerabilities.

- **Best Practices**: Include general security best practices for strengthening the overall security posture, such as implementing strong authentication, regular patching, network segmentation, and regular security audits.

- **Tools and Resources**: If applicable, suggest specific tools or resources that could help in remediating the vulnerabilities (e.g., firewall configuration, endpoint security tools).

7. Proof of Concept (PoC)

Proof of Concept is crucial in demonstrating the exploitability of vulnerabilities. Ethical hackers provide evidence that they were able to exploit the vulnerabilities discovered during testing. PoC should be included when applicable:

- **Code Snippets**: If applicable, show code snippets or payloads used to exploit the vulnerability.
- **Screenshots or Videos**: Visual proof of the exploitation, showing the attacker gaining unauthorized access or exfiltrating data.
- **Exploit Demonstration**: A concise description of the steps followed to exploit the vulnerability (or a link to a recorded demonstration).

8.

This section summarizes the key takeaways from the penetration test, including:

- The overall security posture of the tested system.
- The critical vulnerabilities discovered and their potential impact.
- The next steps for remediating vulnerabilities and improving security.

9. Appendices

The appendices section can include additional information that supports the findings, such as:

- **Network diagrams** or **system architecture** that were analyzed.
- **Detailed logs** or **scripts** used during testing.
- **Full list of tools** used.
- **Glossary of terms** or **acronyms** used in the report.

What to Include: Findings, Recommendations, Proof of Concept

1. Findings

Each vulnerability discovered during penetration testing should be thoroughly described, along with proof that it was successfully exploited. This helps the client understand the severity of each issue and the risk it poses to their business.

- **Example**:
  - **Finding**: SQL Injection in User Login Form
  - **Description**: A SQL injection vulnerability was found in the user login form on the application's website. The application does not properly sanitize user input, allowing an attacker to manipulate the SQL query executed by the application.
  - **Risk**: This vulnerability could allow an attacker to access or modify user credentials, potentially leading to a full system compromise.
  - **Evidence**: Proof-of-concept code demonstrating SQL injection exploitation.
  - **Remediation Advice**: Implement parameterized queries and input validation to prevent SQL injection.

2. Recommendations

For each finding, the report should include a recommendation that helps the organization mitigate or resolve the issue. These recommendations should be practical, actionable, and prioritized based on the severity of the vulnerability.

- **Example**:
  - **Finding**: Weak Password Policy
  - **Recommendation**: Implement a strong password policy, enforcing a minimum length of 12 characters, requiring a combination of uppercase letters,

numbers, and special characters, and mandating password expiration every 90 days.

3. Proof of Concept (PoC)

Providing a proof of concept demonstrates that the vulnerabilities identified are exploitable. This helps clients understand the real-world impact of the vulnerability and how it could be leveraged by an attacker.

- **Example**:
  - **Finding**: Remote Code Execution (RCE) Vulnerability
  - **PoC**: A script was used to upload a malicious payload to the vulnerable server, resulting in arbitrary code execution on the system.

Example of a Well-Written Penetration Testing Report

Penetration Test Report: Web Application Testing for XYZ Corp

Client: XYZ Corporation
Date: January 1, 2025
Penetration Tester: John Doe, Certified Ethical Hacker (CEH)

Executive Summary: This report outlines the findings from the penetration test conducted on XYZ Corp's web application. The goal of the test was to identify vulnerabilities in the application and the underlying infrastructure that could be exploited by attackers. The testing revealed several critical vulnerabilities, including an SQL injection vulnerability in the login form and improper API authentication. Immediate action is recommended to remediate these findings.

Methodology: Testing was conducted in four phases:

1. Information Gathering
2. Vulnerability Scanning and Enumeration
3. Exploitation and Post-Exploitation
4. Reporting and Remediation Recommendations

Tools used during the test include Burp Suite, Nmap, Metasploit, and Nikto.

Findings:

1. **SQL Injection in User Login Form**
   - **Description**: The user login form does not sanitize user input, allowing SQL injection attacks.

- ○ **Risk**: An attacker could bypass authentication or extract sensitive information from the database.
- ○ **Evidence**: A proof-of-concept SQL injection attack was executed, retrieving user credentials.
- ○ **Severity**: Critical

2. **Improper API Authentication**

- ○ **Description**: The API lacks proper authentication mechanisms, allowing unauthorized users to access sensitive endpoints.
- ○ **Risk**: An attacker could use the API to access private data or perform unauthorized actions.
- ○ **Evidence**: Unauthorized API requests were successfully executed without authentication tokens.
- ○ **Severity**: High

Recommendations:

1. **SQL Injection**: Implement parameterized queries and input validation to mitigate SQL injection risks.

2. **API Authentication**: Implement OAuth 2.0 for secure API authentication and ensure that endpoints are properly secured.

: The penetration test revealed significant vulnerabilities in the web application that could lead to severe security breaches. Immediate remediation is recommended to address these issues and secure the application.

Appendices:

- Full Nmap Scan Results
- Screenshots of Exploited Vulnerabilities
- Detailed Attack Scenarios and PoC

A well-written penetration testing report is an essential deliverable that communicates vulnerabilities, risks, and recommendations to the client. The report must be structured to ensure clarity and provide actionable insights. By detailing findings, providing a proof of concept, and recommending specific remediation steps, the penetration tester helps the organization understand the risks and take necessary action to secure their systems.

Chapter 21: Advanced Penetration Testing Techniques

Advanced Methods Like Pivoting, Exploitation Chaining, and Zero-Day Attacks

Penetration testing is a constantly evolving field, and as security measures become more advanced, so too must the methods and techniques used by ethical hackers. Advanced penetration testing techniques allow testers to bypass sophisticated defenses, exploit multiple vulnerabilities in a chain, and identify previously unknown vulnerabilities that can lead to full system compromise. In this chapter, we will explore advanced methods such as pivoting, exploitation chaining, and zero-day attacks, and provide real-world examples and tools used by advanced penetration testers.

1. Pivoting

Pivoting is a technique used in penetration testing to gain access to networks or systems that are otherwise unreachable due to network segmentation or firewalls. When ethical hackers compromise a system inside the target network, they can use it as a "pivot point" to launch attacks against other systems within the same network. This allows the attacker to move laterally and escalate their access privileges within the compromised environment.

- **How Pivoting Works**: After compromising an internal system (e.g., a vulnerable server), the penetration tester uses the compromised system as a stepping stone to gain access to other systems that are not directly exposed to the internet or external attackers. This is often done by setting up a **proxy** or **VPN** on the compromised system that routes traffic to other internal targets.

- **Example**: A penetration tester gains access to a vulnerable web server within a company's intranet. This server has direct access to an internal database. By pivoting through the compromised server, the tester can interact with the database without direct access to it, exploiting vulnerabilities and extracting sensitive data.

- **Tools for Pivoting**:
  - **Metasploit**: Metasploit's **Meterpreter** payload supports pivoting, allowing testers to route traffic through compromised machines.
  - **ProxyChains**: A tool that forces traffic through a chain of proxy servers, which can be useful for pivoting in a penetration test.
  - **SSH Tunneling**: Using SSH to create a secure tunnel between the attacker's system and the compromised machine, enabling access to internal systems.

2. Exploitation Chaining

Exploitation chaining refers to the practice of combining multiple vulnerabilities or attack vectors in a sequence to achieve a more complex or impactful attack. This technique allows penetration testers to escalate privileges, bypass security mechanisms, and ultimately gain deeper access into the target system or network.

- **How Exploitation Chaining Works**: In a typical exploitation chain, a tester might first exploit a vulnerability to gain low-level access to a system. Next, they might exploit another vulnerability to escalate their privileges and gain administrative access. They could then use another vulnerability to access sensitive data or execute arbitrary code on other machines within the network.

- **Example**: A penetration tester might first use a **phishing** attack to gain initial access to a user's system. From there, they could exploit a **privilege escalation** vulnerability to gain administrator rights, followed by using a **misconfigured SMB** service to move laterally across the network, ultimately compromising other machines or servers.

- **Tools for Exploitation Chaining**:
  - **Metasploit**: The **Metasploit Framework** is invaluable for chaining exploits. Testers can automatically apply a series of exploits in a sequence to achieve their objectives.

- o **Cobalt Strike**: A tool designed for advanced penetration testing that supports exploitation chaining, post-exploitation activities, and pivoting.
- o **Burp Suite**: In web application testing, Burp Suite's **Intruder** tool can be used to automate the chaining of exploits like SQL injection and Cross-Site Scripting (XSS) attacks.

3. Zero-Day Attacks

A **zero-day attack** occurs when an attacker exploits a vulnerability that is unknown to the software vendor or security community. Since the vendor has had "zero days" to fix the vulnerability, these attacks are extremely dangerous because there is no immediate fix or mitigation. Zero-day vulnerabilities are highly prized by attackers, and discovering them requires deep knowledge of the target system and software.

- **How Zero-Day Attacks Work**: An attacker discovers a vulnerability in a system or software application that has not yet been publicly disclosed or patched. The attacker exploits this flaw to gain unauthorized access or control of the system. Zero-day attacks are particularly difficult to defend against because no signature or patch exists at the time of the attack.
- **Example**: The **Stuxnet** worm is one of the most famous real-world examples of a zero-day attack. It used multiple zero-day vulnerabilities to infect industrial control systems and

sabotage Iran's nuclear program without being detected by traditional antivirus tools.

- **Tools for Zero-Day Exploitation**:
  - ○ **Immunity Debugger**: A powerful debugger that helps exploit developers identify zero-day vulnerabilities in software applications.
  - ○ **IDA Pro**: A disassembler and debugger used to analyze software binaries and identify potential vulnerabilities that can be exploited, including zero-day vulnerabilities.
  - ○ **CVE Databases**: Zero-day vulnerabilities are often discovered through deep research, and publicly accessible vulnerability databases (such as **CVE** and **Exploit-DB**) can sometimes help ethical hackers identify previously unknown flaws to use in testing.

Real-World Examples of Advanced Penetration Testing

1. The SolarWinds Hack (2020)

In one of the most sophisticated cyberattacks in recent history, hackers compromised the **SolarWinds Orion** software used by thousands of organizations, including U.S. government agencies, defense contractors, and large corporations. This attack leveraged exploitation chaining, pivoting, and advanced persistence mechanisms.

- **Exploitation Chaining**: The attackers first gained access to SolarWinds' internal systems and then injected malicious code into updates for the Orion software. This allowed them to infect the software used by clients.

- **Pivoting and Lateral Movement**: Once inside a client's network, the attackers moved laterally, using **Cobalt Strike** and other tools to pivot through the network and gain deeper access.

- **Zero-Day Exploits**: The attackers used zero-day vulnerabilities in the Orion software to maintain persistence and evade detection, demonstrating the power of zero-day attacks in high-stakes cybersecurity incidents.

2. The WannaCry Ransomware Attack (2017)

The WannaCry ransomware attack used a combination of **exploitation chaining** and **zero-day vulnerabilities** to spread rapidly across networks worldwide. The attack exploited a zero-day vulnerability in Microsoft's **SMBv1** protocol, known as **EternalBlue**, which was originally discovered by the NSA and leaked by the Shadow Brokers group.

- **Exploitation Chaining**: Once inside an organization's network, WannaCry leveraged the EternalBlue exploit to propagate to other systems.
- **Zero-Day Exploit**: The exploit used in WannaCry was a zero-day vulnerability in the Windows SMBv1 protocol. Microsoft had not released a patch for the vulnerability at the time of the attack, making it a dangerous zero-day attack that affected hundreds of thousands of machines globally.

Tools for Advanced Penetration Testers

Advanced penetration testing requires specialized tools that can handle complex attack scenarios, including pivoting, exploitation chaining, and zero-day vulnerabilities. Here are some of the most widely used tools by experienced penetration testers:

1. Metasploit Framework

Metasploit is one of the most comprehensive tools available for penetration testers. It includes a vast database of exploits and post-exploitation modules, which allows testers to chain exploits and pivot through compromised networks. Metasploit also has an integrated payload generation system, making it useful for advanced exploitation.

- **Key Features**:

- o Automatic exploitation of vulnerabilities.
- o Post-exploitation features like pivoting and credential harvesting.
- o Supports **meterpreter**, a payload that provides remote control of a target system.

2. Cobalt Strike

Cobalt Strike is a powerful tool for advanced penetration testers, especially for red team operations. It provides a full set of features for exploitation, lateral movement, persistence, and data exfiltration.

- **Key Features**:
  - o Advanced **Beacon** payload for establishing persistent communication with compromised systems.
  - o Support for **exploitation chaining** and lateral movement.
  - o **Mimikatz** integration for credential dumping and escalation.

3. Burp Suite Professional

Burp Suite is a powerful tool used for web application penetration testing. The professional version offers advanced features like automated vulnerability scanning, crawling, and session handling, which are invaluable when exploiting web application vulnerabilities.

- **Key Features**:
  - **Intruder** tool for automating attacks like brute force and fuzzing.
  - **Repeater** tool for manually modifying and re-sending HTTP requests.
  - **Extensibility** with plugins and integration with other tools.

4. Immunity Debugger

Immunity Debugger is a disassembler and debugger commonly used for vulnerability research and exploit development. It allows testers to analyze software binaries and identify potential vulnerabilities, making it a vital tool for discovering zero-day exploits.

- **Key Features**:
  - Dynamic analysis of binaries.
  - Supports remote debugging, which is helpful for reverse engineering malware and exploits.
  - Highly customizable with the ability to write Python scripts for automating tasks.

5. Wireshark

Wireshark is a network protocol analyzer that allows penetration testers to capture and inspect network traffic in real-time. It's particularly useful for **Man-in-the-Middle (MITM)** attacks and analyzing network-based vulnerabilities.

- **Key Features**:
  - ○ Real-time packet capturing and analysis.
  - ○ Decryption of SSL/TLS traffic (with the appropriate keys).
  - ○ Protocol dissectors for hundreds of network protocols.

Advanced penetration testing techniques, such as **pivoting**, **exploitation chaining**, and **zero-day attacks**, allow ethical hackers to exploit vulnerabilities and gain deeper access to systems in ways that traditional penetration testing methods cannot. These techniques require specialized skills, knowledge, and tools to execute successfully. By leveraging tools like **Metasploit, Cobalt Strike**, and **Burp Suite**, ethical hackers can perform sophisticated testing that uncovers vulnerabilities across systems and networks, even in highly secure environments.

Real-world attacks, such as the **SolarWinds breach** and **WannaCry ransomware**, highlight the importance of advanced penetration testing techniques for identifying and mitigating potential threats. As cyber attackers continue to evolve their tactics, ethical hackers must stay up to date with the latest techniques, tools, and vulnerabilities to help organizations protect their infrastructure from advanced threats.

Chapter 22: Penetration Testing in Different Industries

Customizing Penetration Testing for Different Industries (Finance, Healthcare, Government)

Penetration testing is not a one-size-fits-all activity. Different industries have unique challenges, security requirements, and compliance regulations that influence the approach taken during penetration testing. Ethical hackers must tailor their penetration testing strategies to address the specific needs and vulnerabilities of the industry they are working with.

1. Finance Industry

The **finance industry** includes banks, investment firms, insurance companies, and payment processors. Due to the sensitive nature of financial data and the potential for financial loss, the security of systems in the finance industry is a top priority. Penetration testing in this industry often focuses on protecting customer information, transaction data, and financial assets.

- **Key Focus Areas**:
  - **Payment Systems**: Testing the security of transaction systems, online banking portals, and payment gateways. Vulnerabilities in these systems

can lead to financial fraud or unauthorized access to customer accounts.

- o **Data Encryption**: Ensuring that financial data, both in transit and at rest, is securely encrypted to prevent interception or data breaches.
- o **User Authentication**: Examining the security of authentication mechanisms, such as multi-factor authentication (MFA), to ensure only authorized users can access sensitive financial data.

- **Challenges**:
  - o Financial institutions face complex compliance regulations (e.g., **PCI DSS**, **SOX**, **GLBA**) that require specific security measures.
  - o The ever-evolving threat landscape, including advanced **social engineering** attacks and **insider threats**.

- **Regulations**:
  - o **PCI DSS** (Payment Card Industry Data Security Standard) requires testing for vulnerabilities in payment systems, ensuring compliance with secure card processing and data handling standards.
  - o **SOX** (Sarbanes-Oxley Act) mandates financial reporting and internal control testing to ensure corporate financial integrity.

2. Healthcare Industry

The **healthcare industry** includes hospitals, clinics, pharmaceutical companies, and health insurance providers. Due to the sensitive nature of health data, security in healthcare systems is highly regulated and critical. Penetration testing in the healthcare industry is focused on safeguarding electronic health records (EHRs), patient data, and other confidential medical information.

- **Key Focus Areas**:
    - **Protected Health Information (PHI)**: Ensuring the confidentiality and integrity of PHI, which includes personal details, medical history, and treatment records.
    - **Medical Devices**: Testing the security of Internet of Things (IoT) devices used in medical applications, such as heart rate monitors and insulin pumps. Vulnerabilities in these devices can lead to unauthorized access or manipulation of patient data.
    - **Electronic Health Record (EHR) Systems**: Identifying vulnerabilities in EHR systems that could expose patient data or allow unauthorized access to medical records.
- **Challenges**:
    - Strict privacy regulations such as **HIPAA** (Health Insurance Portability and Accountability Act)

require that all healthcare data is kept confidential and secure.

o Medical devices often have outdated or poorly maintained software, creating additional vulnerabilities.

- **Regulations**:

  o **HIPAA** requires healthcare organizations to implement strong data protection measures and undergo regular penetration testing to ensure the security of patient information.

  o **HITRUST CSF** (Health Information Trust Alliance Common Security Framework) is a certification framework that combines various healthcare-related regulations and standards.

3. Government Sector

Government agencies and contractors are critical to national security and public services. Penetration testing in the government sector focuses on protecting sensitive data, national security information, and critical infrastructure. It also addresses the protection of classified information from both external and internal threats.

- **Key Focus Areas**:

  o **Critical Infrastructure**: Testing government control systems, including water treatment, power grids, transportation, and defense systems, to prevent cyberattacks on vital infrastructure.

- o **Sensitive Government Data**: Protecting classified information, citizen data, and law enforcement records from unauthorized access or leaks.
- o **Cyber Espionage**: Identifying vulnerabilities that could be exploited by foreign state-sponsored actors or hackers attempting to infiltrate government systems for espionage or sabotage.

- **Challenges**:
  - o National security concerns require high levels of secrecy, making it difficult to test certain systems.
  - o Legacy systems, often found in government agencies, are notoriously insecure and difficult to update or patch due to funding and compatibility issues.

- **Regulations**:
  - o **FISMA** (Federal Information Security Modernization Act) mandates that federal agencies and contractors implement robust cybersecurity measures, including regular penetration testing, to protect sensitive government information.
  - o **NIST** (National Institute of Standards and Technology) provides frameworks and guidelines for cybersecurity practices, including penetration testing, for government agencies.

Challenges and Regulations for Specific Industries

Each industry faces unique challenges when it comes to cybersecurity and penetration testing. These challenges often stem from the specific regulatory environments, the type of data handled, and the nature of the attacks that each sector is most vulnerable to. Here are some of the key challenges faced by specific industries:

1. Financial Industry Challenges:

- **Legacy Systems**: Many financial institutions still rely on outdated systems that are difficult to patch or secure. Penetration testers must account for these vulnerabilities when conducting assessments.
- **Compliance with Regulatory Frameworks**: Financial institutions are subject to numerous regulatory requirements, such as **PCI DSS** and **SOX**, which necessitate penetration tests to ensure compliance.

2. Healthcare Industry Challenges:

- **Data Sensitivity**: Patient health data is some of the most sensitive data that exists. Penetration testers must ensure that vulnerabilities in health systems don't expose this information.

- **IoT Device Security**: Medical devices in hospitals are often connected to networks and must be tested for vulnerabilities to ensure that they are not exploited to compromise patient data or harm patients.

- **Regulatory Compliance**: HIPAA compliance is critical in healthcare, and penetration testing must consider how well organizations adhere to the requirements for handling PHI.

3. Government Sector Challenges:

- **National Security**: Government agencies handle highly sensitive and classified data, so penetration testing must ensure that attackers cannot access this information.

- **State-Sponsored Attacks**: Governments are often the target of advanced persistent threats (APTs) from foreign state actors, requiring a different approach to penetration testing.

- **Regulatory Oversight**: Government agencies must comply with standards such as **FISMA** and **NIST** for security testing, adding complexity to the testing process.

Case Studies of Industry-Specific Penetration Testing

1. Target Data Breach (2013) - Retail Industry

One of the most notable security breaches in the retail industry was the **Target data breach** in 2013. The breach was caused by a vulnerability in Target's third-party vendor's network, which allowed attackers to gain access to the retail giant's point-of-sale (POS) systems. The attackers were able to steal over 40 million credit and debit card numbers and 70 million customer records.

- **Penetration Testing Outcome**: The breach was a result of insufficient network segmentation and weak third-party vendor security. Target's systems were not adequately tested for vulnerabilities, and the attackers were able to exploit them by accessing the network through a vendor.
- **Lessons Learned**: Penetration testing should involve not only internal networks but also third-party vendors and external communication channels. Ensuring proper network segmentation and testing external access points are critical to protecting sensitive data.

2. The WannaCry Ransomware Attack (2017) - Healthcare and Government

The **WannaCry** ransomware attack of 2017 affected hundreds of thousands of systems worldwide, including those in the healthcare and government sectors. The ransomware exploited a **zero-day vulnerability** in Microsoft's SMB protocol (EternalBlue) to spread across networks. The NHS (National Health Service) in the UK was severely impacted, with systems being rendered inoperable, causing widespread disruption to patient care.

- **Penetration Testing Outcome**: The attack highlighted the importance of **patching and updating systems** to protect against known vulnerabilities. Penetration testers in the healthcare and government sectors must ensure that all systems are regularly updated and tested for exposure to known exploits like EternalBlue.

- **Lessons Learned**: Regular patching and proactive vulnerability management are crucial for preventing ransomware attacks. Penetration testing should always check for the presence of unpatched vulnerabilities that could lead to such attacks.

3. The Equifax Data Breach (2017) - Financial Industry

In 2017, **Equifax**, one of the largest credit reporting agencies in the U.S., suffered a massive data breach due to a vulnerability in **Apache Struts**—an open-source framework used by Equifax. The breach exposed the personal data of 147 million people, including Social Security numbers, birthdates, and addresses.

- **Penetration Testing Outcome**: The breach occurred because the vulnerability in Apache Struts had been known and a patch had been released months prior to the attack. However, Equifax had failed to apply the patch, leaving its systems exposed.

- **Lessons Learned**: Penetration testing for organizations handling sensitive financial data should include testing for vulnerabilities in third-party software components. Timely patching and regular system updates must be prioritized.

Penetration testing must be tailored to the unique requirements of different industries, considering the specific challenges and regulations that each sector faces. In industries like finance, healthcare, and government, penetration testing is critical to ensuring compliance with regulatory frameworks, protecting sensitive data, and mitigating the risk of sophisticated cyberattacks. By customizing penetration testing approaches to suit the industry's unique needs, ethical hackers can help organizations strengthen their defenses and minimize the impact of potential vulnerabilities.

Penetration testing should not only be seen as a technical exercise but as a strategic activity aimed at identifying and mitigating risks before they can be exploited by malicious actors. Case studies like **Target**, **WannaCry**, and **Equifax** demonstrate how vulnerabilities can lead to significant financial, reputational, and operational damage. By continually refining and adapting penetration testing practices, organizations can better protect themselves in an increasingly connected and threat-laden world.

Chapter 23: Reporting and Communication in Penetration Testing

Best Practices for Communicating Findings to Clients

Effective communication of findings from a penetration test is crucial to ensuring that the results lead to actionable improvements in security. Penetration testers must be able to translate technical findings into clear, understandable language for clients. A well-structured and properly communicated report helps clients understand the risks, prioritize remediation efforts, and make informed decisions.

1. Tailor the Report to the Audience

Different stakeholders within the organization may need different types of information. When preparing a penetration testing report, it's important to consider the audience and adjust the level of detail accordingly.

- **Non-Technical Stakeholders (e.g., executives, management)**: Focus on high-level summaries of the security posture, risks, and actionable recommendations. Avoid technical jargon and emphasize the business impact of each vulnerability.
- **Technical Stakeholders (e.g., IT security teams, system administrators)**: Provide detailed technical information,

including proof of concepts, specific vulnerabilities, and in-depth remediation steps.

2. Be Clear and Concise

Penetration testing reports should avoid excessive technical details unless they are necessary for technical teams. Use **clear, concise language** to communicate the findings, and ensure that the report is easily digestible.

- **Use Bullet Points and Visual Aids**: Bullet points, tables, and charts help break down information, making it easier to read and understand.
- **Executive Summary**: Start the report with a brief summary that highlights key findings and recommendations, providing a snapshot of the most critical issues.

3. Quantify Risk

Risk quantification is vital for helping clients prioritize remediation. Rather than simply listing vulnerabilities, include a risk assessment that indicates the likelihood of exploitation and the potential impact on the organization.

- **Severity Ratings**: Classify vulnerabilities using severity ratings such as **Critical**, **High**, **Medium**, or **Low**, helping clients prioritize based on the potential business impact.

- **Risk Matrix**: Provide a risk matrix that shows the severity of each vulnerability alongside its likelihood of being exploited.

4. Actionable Recommendations

For each identified vulnerability, provide **clear, actionable recommendations** that the client can implement to resolve the issue. Be specific and provide guidance on how to mitigate the risk. Also, ensure that the recommendations are feasible and take into account the client's environment and resources.

5. Follow Up

Penetration testing is not a one-time event. Following up with the client is essential to ensure that vulnerabilities have been addressed. Offering support for remediation, additional testing, or advice on improving the security posture after the test is a value-added service.

How to Write a Report That Non-Technical Stakeholders Can Understand

While technical stakeholders need a detailed technical analysis of the findings, non-technical stakeholders such as executives, managers, or legal teams need to understand the **business impact** of the vulnerabilities identified in the penetration test. Below are key strategies for making a penetration testing report accessible and actionable for non-technical stakeholders:

1. Executive Summary

The executive summary should be at the beginning of the report and serve as a concise, non-technical overview of the penetration test. It should be brief (1–2 pages) and summarize the most important findings, risks, and business implications. This section should answer the following questions:

- What was tested and why?
- What were the most critical vulnerabilities found?
- What are the business impacts of these vulnerabilities?
- What should be done next to address the findings?

2. Avoid Technical Jargon

While it may be tempting to use technical language in the report, avoid overwhelming non-technical readers with jargon. Instead, focus on explaining technical terms in layman's language and emphasize the impact of the issues. For example:

- **Technical Term**: "SQL injection vulnerability"
- **Non-Technical Explanation**: "A flaw in the website's code that could allow an attacker to access the customer database, potentially exposing sensitive customer information such as credit card details."

3. Use Analogies and Visuals

Non-technical stakeholders often better understand complex concepts when they are presented using **analogies** or **visual aids**. Analogies simplify difficult concepts, while visuals like **graphs**, **charts**, and **tables** can make the report more engaging and easier to digest.

- **Example Analogy**: "An unpatched system is like leaving the front door of a house unlocked—anyone could walk in."
- **Visuals**: Use **pie charts** to show the distribution of vulnerabilities by severity or **bar charts** to highlight the number of vulnerabilities across different systems.

4. Focus on the Business Impact

Rather than just listing technical issues, focus on explaining the potential **business impact** of each vulnerability. For example:

- **Vulnerability**: Unpatched web application
- **Business Impact**: "An attacker could exploit this vulnerability to steal customer data, resulting in financial loss, reputational damage, and legal consequences from non-compliance with data protection regulations."

5. Prioritize Recommendations

Provide **prioritized recommendations** that help the client understand which vulnerabilities need to be addressed first. This will help non-technical stakeholders make informed decisions about the next steps and allocate resources accordingly.

Example of a Penetration Testing Report with Actionable Recommendations

Penetration   Testing   Report   for   XYZ   Corp.
Client: XYZ   Corporation
Date: January   15,   2025
Penetration Tester: John Doe, Certified Ethical Hacker (CEH)

Executive Summary

This report outlines the findings from the penetration test conducted on XYZ Corp's internal and external web applications. The primary objective was to identify vulnerabilities that could be exploited by attackers to gain unauthorized access or compromise sensitive data.

Key Findings:

- **SQL Injection vulnerability** in the login form, allowing attackers to bypass authentication.
- **Outdated SSL certificates**, exposing the website to Man-in-the-Middle (MITM) attacks.

- **Weak password policy**, enabling easy brute force attacks on user accounts.

Business Impact:

- The **SQL Injection** vulnerability could allow attackers to access sensitive customer data, such as credit card information, potentially leading to a significant data breach.
- The **outdated SSL certificates** expose the company to MITM attacks, where attackers could intercept sensitive customer information during transactions.
- The **weak password policy** increases the risk of unauthorized access to internal systems, potentially allowing attackers to escalate privileges and compromise corporate data.

Methodology

The penetration testing process included the following phases:

1. **Information Gathering**: Scanning for open ports, services, and vulnerabilities.
2. **Vulnerability Assessment**: Scanning for known vulnerabilities in applications, services, and configurations.
3. **Exploitation**: Attempting to exploit identified vulnerabilities to gain unauthorized access.

4. **Post-Exploitation**: Attempting to escalate privileges and extract sensitive data.

5. **Reporting**: Documenting findings and providing actionable recommendations.

Findings

1. **SQL Injection in User Login Form**
   - o **Description**: The login form on the corporate website is vulnerable to SQL injection attacks, which could allow an attacker to bypass authentication and gain access to user accounts.
   - o **Risk Level: Critical**
   - o **Evidence**: The tester successfully executed a SQL injection payload and gained access to the database.
   - o **Recommendation**: Implement parameterized queries to prevent SQL injection attacks. Sanitize all user inputs to ensure they cannot manipulate SQL queries.

2. **Outdated SSL Certificates**
   - o **Description**: The SSL certificates for the website are outdated, exposing the company to MITM attacks.
   - o **Risk Level: High**

- o **Evidence**: The SSL certificates were found to be expired, and traffic was transmitted over HTTP rather than HTTPS.
- o **Recommendation**: Renew SSL certificates immediately and enforce HTTPS across the entire website to encrypt communication and prevent MITM attacks.

3. **Weak Password Policy**

- o **Description**: The current password policy allows for weak passwords, which can be easily cracked using brute force techniques.
- o **Risk Level: Medium**
- o **Evidence**: The tester was able to crack several user passwords within a few minutes using automated brute force tools.
- o **Recommendation**: Implement a strong password policy requiring at least 12 characters, a mix of upper and lowercase letters, numbers, and special characters. Additionally, enforce multi-factor authentication (MFA) for all sensitive accounts.

This penetration test identified several critical vulnerabilities in XYZ Corp's web application and internal security practices.

Immediate action is required to address these issues and reduce the risk of data breaches or cyberattacks. The following steps should be prioritized:

1. Fix the SQL injection vulnerability in the login form.
2. Renew SSL certificates and enforce HTTPS.
3. Strengthen the password policy and enforce MFA.

Appendices

- Full Nmap Scan Results
- Screenshots of Exploited Vulnerabilities
- Detailed Attack Scenarios

Writing a penetration testing report is not just about documenting technical findings—it's about communicating risks and providing actionable recommendations to improve the client's security posture. A well-structured report helps both technical and non-technical stakeholders understand the vulnerabilities, their business impact, and the necessary steps for remediation. By following best practices for communication, penetration testers can ensure that their findings are both informative and actionable, leading to meaningful improvements in the organization's security.

Chapter 24: Mitigating Cybersecurity Risks After Testing

Steps to Mitigate Vulnerabilities After a Penetration Test

Once a penetration test is completed and vulnerabilities have been identified, the next crucial step is to mitigate those vulnerabilities effectively. Mitigation ensures that the discovered weaknesses are addressed in a timely manner to reduce the risk of exploitation. Below are key steps to take in mitigating vulnerabilities after a penetration test:

1. Prioritize Vulnerabilities

Not all vulnerabilities pose the same level of risk to an organization. Some may be critical and can lead to severe consequences if exploited, while others may be less impactful. After receiving the results of the penetration test, organizations should prioritize the vulnerabilities based on their **severity**, **likelihood of exploitation**, and **potential impact** on business operations.

- **Critical vulnerabilities** should be addressed immediately, such as those that allow remote code execution, unauthorized access to sensitive data, or privilege escalation.
- **Medium and low vulnerabilities** can be addressed later, but they should still be part of the organization's remediation plan.

2. Develop an Action Plan

Once vulnerabilities are prioritized, an **action plan** should be created to define specific steps for remediation. This includes assigning responsibilities to the appropriate teams (e.g., network administrators, developers, IT security personnel), setting timelines for resolving the issues, and tracking progress.

- **Assign Ownership**: Each vulnerability should have an assigned owner, typically someone with the expertise and access required to address the issue (e.g., system administrators for patching systems, developers for application flaws).
- **Set Timelines**: Establish realistic deadlines for fixing the vulnerabilities. For high-severity vulnerabilities, remediation should be done as soon as possible (within days or weeks).

3. Remediate and Patch Systems

System patching is one of the most important aspects of vulnerability mitigation. Many of the vulnerabilities discovered during a penetration test can be resolved by applying patches to software, operating systems, and firmware.

- **Patch Operating Systems and Software**: Ensure all systems are up-to-date with the latest security patches from vendors. This applies to both desktop and server operating systems, as well as applications.

- **Fix Configuration Issues**: Many vulnerabilities are the result of misconfigurations. These should be addressed by reviewing configuration settings, changing default passwords, and enforcing security best practices.

- **Close Open Ports**: Ensure that unnecessary network services are disabled and that open ports are secured or closed.

4. Test the Fixes

After implementing patches and fixes, organizations should test the systems again to ensure that the vulnerabilities have been effectively mitigated and that no new issues have been introduced. This process, called **retesting**, ensures that the fixes are working as expected.

- **Automated Testing Tools**: Use vulnerability scanning tools to confirm that the patched systems are no longer vulnerable to the same exploits.

- **Manual Validation**: In some cases, manual verification may be needed, especially for complex issues that require more than just a software patch (e.g., business logic vulnerabilities in applications).

5. Implement Security Controls and Hardening

In addition to patching vulnerabilities, organizations should implement **security controls** and **hardening measures** to reduce the risk of future exploitation. This can include:

- **Firewall and IDS/IPS**: Ensure that firewalls and intrusion detection/prevention systems (IDS/IPS) are configured correctly to monitor and block malicious activity.
- **Least Privilege**: Ensure that users and systems have only the minimum level of access necessary to perform their tasks (the principle of least privilege).
- **Multi-Factor Authentication (MFA)**: Implement MFA to add an extra layer of security, especially for accessing critical systems or sensitive data.

6. Monitor for New Vulnerabilities

Mitigating existing vulnerabilities is only part of the process; continuous monitoring is critical for identifying new vulnerabilities and threats. Regular vulnerability assessments, system audits, and penetration testing should be conducted to stay ahead of emerging risks.

- **Continuous Monitoring**: Use tools like **SIEM** (Security Information and Event Management) systems to track logs and monitor for unusual activity.

- **Periodic Penetration Testing**: Penetration tests should be performed on a regular basis to identify new vulnerabilities, especially after significant changes to systems or software.

Best Practices for Patch Management and Continuous Monitoring

1. Patch Management Best Practices

Patch management is a vital part of any organization's cybersecurity strategy. It ensures that systems are kept up-to-date with the latest security fixes to prevent vulnerabilities from being exploited by attackers.

- **Establish a Patch Management Policy**: Define clear guidelines for when patches should be applied, how they should be tested, and who is responsible for applying them.
- **Automate Patching**: Where possible, automate patch deployment to reduce the time it takes to apply fixes. Use tools like **WSUS** (Windows Server Update Services) or third-party patch management software to automate patching on all systems.
- **Test Patches Before Deployment**: Before applying patches to production systems, test them in a controlled environment

to ensure they don't cause system instability or compatibility issues.

- **Track Patches**: Keep track of which patches have been applied and which systems are up-to-date. Use patch management software to automate tracking and generate reports.

2. Continuous Monitoring Best Practices

Continuous monitoring is critical for identifying potential threats and vulnerabilities in real-time. By implementing continuous monitoring strategies, organizations can detect and respond to incidents before they escalate into major security breaches.

- **Real-Time Network Monitoring**: Use network monitoring tools (e.g., **Wireshark**, **Nagios**) to analyze traffic and detect unusual patterns that could indicate a security threat.
- **Log Management and Analysis**: Ensure that logs from all critical systems (e.g., firewalls, servers, and applications) are collected, stored, and analyzed regularly using a **SIEM** system.
- **Behavioral Analytics**: Implement **User and Entity Behavior Analytics (UEBA)** tools to monitor user activity and detect deviations from normal behavior, which may indicate compromised accounts or insider threats.

- **Threat Intelligence**: Leverage threat intelligence feeds and services to stay informed about emerging vulnerabilities and exploits that may affect your organization.

Real-World Example of How Mitigation Strategies Helped a Company

Example: The WannaCry Ransomware Attack and Mitigation Strategies

In 2017, the **WannaCry** ransomware attack affected organizations worldwide, including healthcare institutions, telecom companies, and government agencies. The attack exploited a **zero-day vulnerability** in the **Microsoft Windows SMBv1** protocol (EternalBlue), affecting hundreds of thousands of systems. However, many organizations that had applied Microsoft's security patches were able to mitigate the damage and avoid being affected by the attack.

- **Mitigation Strategy**: Microsoft had released a security patch two months before the WannaCry outbreak, but many organizations had not yet deployed it. Organizations that had established strong **patch management policies** and **automated patching systems** were able to quickly deploy the patch across their systems.

- **Outcome**: Companies with continuous monitoring in place were able to detect unusual network traffic related to the ransomware and take action before the malware spread across their networks. Additionally, companies that had implemented strong **backups** were able to restore affected systems without paying the ransom.

The **key takeaway** from this example is that patch management and continuous monitoring were crucial in preventing or mitigating the impact of the WannaCry ransomware attack. Organizations that maintained up-to-date systems and had the proper security controls in place were able to respond swiftly and minimize the damage.

Mitigating vulnerabilities after a penetration test is a critical step in improving an organization's overall security posture. By prioritizing vulnerabilities, developing an action plan, patching systems, and implementing continuous monitoring, organizations can reduce their exposure to cyber risks and prevent future security incidents.

Patch management and continuous monitoring are essential for maintaining a secure environment, ensuring that vulnerabilities are addressed as soon as they are discovered, and that new threats are detected and responded to in real time. The WannaCry attack serves as a stark reminder of the importance of these mitigation strategies and how proactive measures can help organizations defend against rapidly evolving cyber threats. By adopting best practices and regularly testing security measures, organizations can better protect themselves against the ever-growing landscape of cyber threats.

Chapter 25: Ethical Hacking Certifications and Career Pathways

Overview of Certifications (CEH, OSCP, etc.)

Ethical hacking and penetration testing require specialized knowledge and skills, and one of the best ways to demonstrate proficiency in these fields is by obtaining recognized certifications. Certifications serve as a way for professionals to prove their expertise, keep up with the latest developments in cybersecurity, and enhance their career prospects. Below are some of the most widely recognized certifications in ethical hacking:

1. Certified Ethical Hacker (CEH)

The **Certified Ethical Hacker (CEH)** certification, offered by EC-Council, is one of the most recognized certifications in ethical hacking. It is designed for professionals who want to learn how to think and act like a hacker in order to understand how to defend against cyberattacks.

- **Topics Covered**:
    - Ethical hacking concepts and methodologies
    - Footprinting and reconnaissance
    - Scanning networks and enumeration
    - Vulnerability analysis
    - Web application hacking

- o Social engineering
- o Cryptography and malware analysis
- **Who Should Pursue It**: IT security professionals, network administrators, and system engineers who are looking to advance their knowledge of ethical hacking and cybersecurity defenses.
- **Exam**: The CEH exam consists of 125 multiple-choice questions, covering a broad range of topics related to hacking tools and techniques.

2. Offensive Security Certified Professional (OSCP)

The **Offensive Security Certified Professional (OSCP)** is one of the most prestigious certifications for penetration testers and ethical hackers. Offered by **Offensive Security**, the OSCP certification is known for its practical approach, requiring candidates to demonstrate their skills by exploiting vulnerabilities in a controlled environment.

- **Topics Covered**:
  - o Penetration testing methodologies
  - o Web application exploitation
  - o Buffer overflows
  - o Cryptography
  - o Privilege escalation techniques
  - o Bypassing security measures

- **Who Should Pursue It**: The OSCP is designed for more experienced individuals with a solid understanding of penetration testing techniques. It's a great certification for those who want to develop hands-on skills.

- **Exam**: The OSCP exam involves a 24-hour practical test, where candidates must exploit a series of vulnerabilities in a virtual environment, with the goal of gaining administrative access to the target system.

3. Certified Penetration Testing Engineer (CPTE)

The **Certified Penetration Testing Engineer (CPTE)** certification, offered by the **EC-Council**, focuses on the tools and techniques used to conduct penetration testing in a professional and ethical manner. The CPTE exam is designed for individuals looking to demonstrate a thorough understanding of ethical hacking and penetration testing.

- **Topics Covered**:
    - Penetration testing tools
    - Vulnerability scanning
    - Network penetration testing
    - Web application testing
    - Reporting and documentation
    - Security protocols

- **Who Should Pursue It**: Professionals with experience in IT security who want to enhance their skills in penetration testing.

4. Certified Information Systems Security Professional (CISSP)

The **Certified Information Systems Security Professional (CISSP)** is an advanced-level certification for professionals working in IT security. While not specifically focused on ethical hacking, CISSP covers a broad range of topics essential for building a comprehensive security program, including risk management, security architecture, and incident response.

- **Topics Covered**:
    - Security and risk management
    - Asset security
    - Security engineering
    - Communication and network security
    - Identity and access management
- **Who Should Pursue It**: Professionals looking to move into managerial or leadership roles in cybersecurity.

5. CompTIA Security+

The **CompTIA Security+** certification is a foundational certification in cybersecurity that covers a broad range of topics relevant to ethical hackers. It's an excellent starting point for those new to the field of cybersecurity and ethical hacking.

- **Topics Covered**:
  - o Threats and vulnerabilities
  - o Risk management
  - o Network security
  - o Cryptography and public key infrastructure (PKI)
  - o Identity and access management
- **Who Should Pursue It**: Beginners in IT and cybersecurity looking to gain foundational knowledge.

Career Opportunities in Ethical Hacking and Penetration Testing

The demand for skilled ethical hackers and penetration testers has increased significantly in recent years due to the growing frequency and sophistication of cyberattacks. With the increasing reliance on digital systems and the rise of cybercrime, organizations need skilled professionals to safeguard their data and systems.

1. Penetration Tester

Penetration testers, or "ethical hackers," are responsible for simulating cyberattacks to identify vulnerabilities in systems, networks, and applications. They use the same tools and techniques as malicious hackers but do so ethically, with the goal of strengthening security.

- **Key Responsibilities**:
  - o Conduct penetration tests on web applications, networks, and systems
  - o Identify and exploit vulnerabilities
  - o Report findings and recommend remediation steps
  - o Collaborate with IT security teams to patch vulnerabilities
- **Skills Required**:
  - o Knowledge of penetration testing methodologies
  - o Familiarity with ethical hacking tools (e.g., Metasploit, Burp Suite)
  - o Knowledge of operating systems, networks, and application security
  - o Ability to write detailed reports and communicate findings

2. Security Consultant

Security consultants provide expert advice to organizations on how to protect their assets and mitigate security risks. In this role, ethical hacking skills are used to assess the security posture of a client's systems and to provide guidance on best practices.

- **Key Responsibilities**:
  - o Assess and analyze client systems for vulnerabilities
  - o Advise on security policies and practices
  - o Develop risk management strategies

- o Conduct vulnerability assessments and penetration tests
- • **Skills Required**:
  - o In-depth knowledge of cybersecurity practices and frameworks
  - o Strong communication and interpersonal skills
  - o Experience with security audits and risk assessments

3. Security Analyst

Security analysts are responsible for monitoring and protecting an organization's IT infrastructure. They use a variety of tools and techniques, including penetration testing, to detect, prevent, and respond to cyber threats.

- • **Key Responsibilities**:
  - o Monitor systems for signs of potential security incidents
  - o Conduct vulnerability assessments and penetration tests
  - o Investigate and respond to security incidents
  - o Implement and enforce security policies
- • **Skills Required**:
  - o Knowledge of network security, firewalls, and intrusion detection/prevention systems (IDS/IPS)
  - o Familiarity with SIEM tools and threat intelligence feeds

  o Strong analytical and problem-solving skills

4. Incident Responder

Incident responders are tasked with investigating and mitigating the effects of cybersecurity breaches. They work to identify the source and impact of incidents, contain them, and develop strategies to prevent future attacks.

- **Key Responsibilities**:
  - o Respond to security incidents and breaches
  - o Conduct forensic investigations to determine the cause of an attack
  - o Work with other teams to recover from incidents
  - o Develop and implement incident response plans
- **Skills Required**:
  - o Expertise in forensic analysis and incident management
  - o Knowledge of common attack vectors and mitigation techniques
  - o Ability to analyze logs and network traffic to trace intrusions

5. Bug Bounty Hunter

Bug bounty hunters are independent researchers who search for vulnerabilities in applications, websites, or systems. They report discovered vulnerabilities to the organization in exchange for a monetary reward or recognition.

- **Key Responsibilities**:
    - o Search for and report vulnerabilities in applications or websites
    - o Participate in bug bounty programs offered by organizations
    - o Document vulnerabilities and suggest mitigation strategies
- **Skills Required**:
    - o Advanced knowledge of web application security and common vulnerabilities (e.g., XSS, SQL injection)
    - o Familiarity with bug bounty platforms (e.g., HackerOne, Bugcrowd)
    - o Strong understanding of ethical hacking tools and techniques

---

How to Build a Successful Career as an Ethical Hacker

Building a successful career in ethical hacking requires a combination of technical skills, certifications, hands-on experience, and continuous learning. Below are the steps to help you build a rewarding career in ethical hacking:

1. Acquire the Necessary Knowledge

Start by gaining a strong understanding of computer systems, networking, and security principles. Study the basics of operating systems (Linux, Windows), networking protocols (TCP/IP, DNS, HTTP), and programming/scripting (Python, Bash, PowerShell).

- **Recommended Learning Resources**:
  - Online courses (e.g., Coursera, Udemy, Cybrary)
  - Books on ethical hacking, penetration testing, and cybersecurity (e.g., "The Web Application Hacker's Handbook")
  - Labs and challenges on platforms like **Hack The Box** and **TryHackMe**

2. Get Certified

Pursue industry-recognized certifications like **CEH**, **OSCP**, and **CompTIA Security**+ to validate your skills and knowledge. Certifications demonstrate your expertise to potential employers and clients.

- **Start with foundational certifications** (e.g., **CompTIA Security**+ or **Certified Ethical Hacker (CEH)**) and progress to more advanced ones (e.g., **OSCP** or **CISSP**).

3. Gain Hands-On Experience

Hands-on experience is critical in ethical hacking. Set up a home lab to practice penetration testing on virtual machines or vulnerable applications. Participate in **bug bounty programs** or work on real-world challenges to gain practical skills.

- **Tools to Practice**:
  - Virtual machines with tools like **Kali Linux** or **Parrot Security OS**
  - Vulnerable systems like **Metasploitable** or **OWASP Juice Shop**
  - Capture the Flag (CTF) challenges on platforms like **Hack The Box**

4. Join the Ethical Hacking Community

Networking with other cybersecurity professionals can help you learn from others, stay updated on industry trends, and open doors to job opportunities. Join online forums, attend conferences (e.g., **DEFCON, Black Hat**), and contribute to open-source security projects.

- **Communities to Join**:
  - **Reddit's r/netsec or r/AskNetsec**
  - Security forums like **SecurityFocus** and **Stack Overflow**
  - Twitter and LinkedIn for following industry experts

5. *Keep Learning*

Cybersecurity is an ever-evolving field, so it's important to stay up-to-date with the latest techniques, vulnerabilities, and trends. Follow blogs, attend webinars, and continuously challenge yourself with new penetration testing scenarios.

- **Learning Platforms**:
  - **OWASP** for web security standards
  - **SANS Institute** for advanced training
  - **Pluralsight** and **LinkedIn Learning** for ongoing professional development

Ethical hacking is a dynamic and rewarding career path, with a wide range of certifications and career opportunities. From penetration testing and bug bounty hunting to incident response and security consulting, the demand for skilled ethical hackers continues to grow. By obtaining certifications, gaining hands-on experience, and continuously learning, you can build a successful career in ethical hacking and cybersecurity. With the right skills, knowledge, and certifications, you can help organizations stay secure in the face of an ever-evolving threat landscape.

Chapter 26: Future Trends in Ethical Hacking and Cybersecurity

Emerging Threats and Technologies in Cybersecurity

As technology continues to evolve, so do the threats in the cybersecurity landscape. The growing reliance on digital systems and the increasing complexity of cyberattacks mean that ethical hackers must stay vigilant to protect sensitive data and systems. Below are some of the **emerging threats** and **technologies** in cybersecurity that ethical hackers will need to focus on in the coming years.

1. Artificial Intelligence (AI) and Machine Learning (ML) in Cybersecurity

AI and machine learning are already playing a significant role in both the defense and offense of cybersecurity. On one hand, security tools powered by AI can analyze large volumes of data to detect patterns and anomalies, making them effective in identifying potential threats and vulnerabilities.

- **Emerging Threats**:
  - **AI-Powered Attacks**: Attackers are starting to use AI and machine learning to automate attacks, such as phishing or social engineering, by analyzing patterns in human behavior. AI-driven malware can adapt and

modify its code to evade traditional signature-based detection systems.

- **Deepfakes**: The use of AI to create realistic fake videos, images, or audio files (known as **deepfakes**) can be used to launch **social engineering attacks**. For example, attackers may impersonate high-ranking executives to trick employees into transferring money or sharing sensitive information.

- **Defense Opportunities**:
  - AI and ML can also be used for defense by enhancing **intrusion detection systems (IDS)**, **predictive threat analysis**, and **automated response** to security incidents. These technologies enable security teams to detect and respond to attacks in real-time.

2. Internet of Things (IoT) Security

The **Internet of Things (IoT)** is rapidly expanding, with billions of connected devices already in use. However, many of these devices have poor security measures, making them prime targets for cybercriminals. As more critical infrastructure, healthcare devices, and personal data are integrated into IoT ecosystems, the potential for large-scale attacks increases.

- **Emerging Threats**:

- o **Botnets**: IoT devices are often used in botnet attacks, as seen with the **Mirai botnet**. Attackers exploit vulnerable IoT devices to launch **DDoS (Distributed Denial-of-Service)** attacks, causing massive disruptions.

- o **IoT Exploits**: As IoT devices handle sensitive data, attackers could exploit vulnerabilities in connected devices to steal personal data, control devices, or even disrupt critical services like healthcare or transportation.

- **Defense Opportunities**:
  - o Ethical hackers will need to focus on securing IoT devices, which may involve performing penetration tests on devices, networks, and cloud systems to uncover vulnerabilities before malicious actors can exploit them.

3. Cloud Security and Cloud-Native Attacks

With the rise of cloud computing, organizations are increasingly adopting cloud-based infrastructure and services. This has introduced new challenges in securing data, applications, and networks. As more organizations migrate to cloud-native architectures, the attack surface expands.

- **Emerging Threats**:

- o **Misconfigurations**: A major source of security breaches in cloud environments is improper configurations of cloud services, such as databases or access control settings, which leave critical systems exposed.

- o **API Exploits**: Cloud services heavily rely on APIs for communication between applications. Attackers can exploit vulnerabilities in APIs to gain unauthorized access to cloud resources.

- o **Supply Chain Attacks**: Attackers may target the software supply chain by compromising software updates or cloud service providers, allowing them to infiltrate an organization's infrastructure.

- **Defense Opportunities**:
  - o Penetration testers will be needed to test cloud environments for vulnerabilities, with a particular focus on **API security**, **data encryption**, and **access management**.

4. Quantum Computing and Cryptography

Quantum computing holds the promise of revolutionizing many areas of technology, but it also presents a significant challenge to cybersecurity. Quantum computers have the potential to break the encryption algorithms that secure data today, leading to the need for **quantum-resistant cryptography**.

- **Emerging Threats**:
    - **Quantum Decryption**: As quantum computing matures, current cryptographic methods (such as RSA and ECC) may become obsolete. Attackers with access to quantum computers could potentially break traditional encryption and access sensitive data.
    - **Post-Quantum Attacks**: Although quantum computers are not yet widely available, governments, organizations, and hackers are already researching ways to exploit the potential weaknesses of today's encryption algorithms.
- **Defense Opportunities**:
    - The development and adoption of **quantum-safe cryptography** will be necessary to future-proof systems. Ethical hackers will play a crucial role in testing the security of new encryption algorithms against quantum decryption methods.

The Future of Ethical Hacking Tools and Techniques

As new technologies and threats continue to emerge, so too will the tools and techniques used by ethical hackers. The evolution of cybersecurity tools is critical to staying ahead of attackers and mitigating emerging threats. Here are some trends and innovations in the tools and techniques used by penetration testers and ethical hackers:

1. AI-Powered Penetration Testing Tools

With the increasing capabilities of AI and machine learning, penetration testing tools are becoming more intelligent. These tools are capable of automating many aspects of penetration testing, identifying patterns in vulnerabilities, and predicting potential attack vectors.

- **Example**: Tools like **Cobalt Strike** and **Metasploit** are integrating more AI-driven features, enabling penetration testers to automate tasks such as vulnerability discovery, exploit execution, and post-exploitation.

2. Automation and DevSecOps

As organizations adopt **DevSecOps** (Development, Security, and Operations), security is being integrated into the software development lifecycle. This shift means that ethical hackers must focus on **automated security testing** and work closely with development teams to secure applications in real-time.

- **Example**: Continuous integration and continuous deployment (CI/CD) pipelines will include automated security checks that ethical hackers can test, including vulnerability scanning and static code analysis.

3. Advanced Malware Analysis Tools

With the rise of sophisticated malware, ethical hackers will need more advanced malware analysis tools to identify and mitigate new threats. These tools will leverage AI and sandboxing techniques to analyze how malware behaves in real time.

- **Example**: Tools like **Cuckoo Sandbox** and **IDA Pro** are continuously evolving to analyze increasingly complex malware variants and provide penetration testers with insights into how malware spreads and operates within systems.

4. Cloud-Native Penetration Testing Tools

As organizations shift towards cloud environments, penetration testing tools are evolving to meet the challenges of testing cloud-native applications and infrastructures.

- **Example**: Tools like **CloudSploit** and **Pacu** focus on testing cloud environments for vulnerabilities, including misconfigurations and security flaws specific to services like AWS, Azure, and GCP.

How to Stay Up-to-Date in a Constantly Evolving Field

The cybersecurity landscape is always evolving, which means that ethical hackers must continuously update their knowledge and skills to stay ahead of emerging threats. Here are some ways to ensure that you stay current in the ever-changing field of ethical hacking:

1. Continuous Learning

- **Take Online Courses**: Websites like **Udemy**, **Coursera**, and **Cybrary** offer a wealth of cybersecurity courses, from foundational knowledge to advanced techniques.
- **Attend Webinars and Conferences**: Events like **Black Hat**, **DEF CON**, and **RSA Conference** provide opportunities to learn from experts in the field, gain insights into new trends, and network with other professionals.
- **Certifications**: Earning certifications like **CEH**, **OSCP**, and **CISSP** will not only help you stay up to date with industry standards but also provide recognition for your expertise.

2. Participate in Capture the Flag (CTF) Challenges
Participating in **CTF competitions** is a great way to sharpen your skills and stay ahead of the latest techniques in ethical hacking. These challenges provide hands-on experience with a variety of attack vectors and require real-time problem-solving skills.

- **CTF Platforms**:
    - **Hack The Box**
    - **TryHackMe**

o **Root Me**

3. Engage with the Cybersecurity Community

Being active in the cybersecurity community helps you stay informed about the latest vulnerabilities, attack methods, and security tools.

- **Follow Industry Experts** on social media platforms like Twitter and LinkedIn.
- **Contribute to Open Source Projects**: Contributing to projects such as **OWASP** or **Metasploit** can deepen your understanding of current security tools and techniques.
- **Join Forums**: Participate in cybersecurity forums like **Reddit's r/netsec** or **Stack Overflow** to stay informed about the latest industry news.

4. Experiment with New Tools and Techniques

As new tools and techniques emerge, ethical hackers should experiment with them in a lab environment. Set up a **home lab** with virtual machines to simulate different attack scenarios and learn how to use new tools effectively.

The future of ethical hacking and cybersecurity is filled with exciting opportunities, driven by emerging technologies, new threats, and evolving attack techniques. Ethical hackers will need to stay agile, continuously learning and adapting to combat cyber threats. By embracing new tools and techniques, staying up-to-date on emerging threats, and engaging with the cybersecurity community, ethical hackers can continue to play a vital role in securing digital infrastructures.

The key to success in this constantly evolving field is a commitment to **lifelong learning**, hands-on experience, and proactive engagement with the latest advancements in the cybersecurity world. Whether it's staying informed about AI-driven attacks, mastering cloud security, or preparing for the impact of quantum computing, ethical hackers must remain at the forefront of cybersecurity to protect the digital world from ever-evolving threats.

Chapter 27: : Ethical Hacking and Its Importance in Cybersecurity

The Evolving Role of Ethical Hackers

As technology continues to advance, the role of **ethical hackers** has become more critical than ever in securing digital infrastructure. Ethical hackers, or penetration testers, are tasked with identifying vulnerabilities in systems, networks, and applications before malicious actors can exploit them. Their role has evolved alongside the rapid growth of the internet, the proliferation of IoT devices, and the increasing complexity of cyber threats.

Ethical hackers today not only conduct manual penetration tests but also leverage advanced tools, automation, and artificial intelligence to stay ahead of sophisticated attackers. The expanding attack surface, driven by cloud computing, mobile applications, and IoT devices, requires ethical hackers to continuously adapt to new technologies and attack vectors.

Moreover, as businesses and organizations transition to digital-first models, cybersecurity is no longer an optional measure but an essential component of any organization's strategy. Ethical hackers must stay up-to-date with the latest techniques, continuously test systems, and work with other security teams to ensure proactive protection against cyber threats.

Key Developments in the Role of Ethical Hackers:

- **Proactive Security**: Ethical hackers now play a key role in proactively identifying and mitigating risks before they turn into full-blown attacks.
- **Collaboration with Developers**: Ethical hackers increasingly work alongside software developers and IT teams to incorporate security practices early in the development process, reducing vulnerabilities in the code.
- **Focus on Cloud and IoT Security**: With the growing adoption of cloud computing and IoT devices, ethical hackers are expanding their skill sets to address vulnerabilities in these new environments.
- **Automation and AI**: Ethical hackers are adopting automation tools powered by AI to improve the speed and accuracy of vulnerability detection.

Why Ethical Hacking Is Essential for Modern Cybersecurity

The digital age has transformed every aspect of our lives, from how we communicate and work to how we manage our finances and healthcare. As businesses, governments, and individuals rely more heavily on technology, the potential for cyber threats has grown exponentially. In this environment, **ethical hacking** plays a vital role in ensuring the security of digital systems.

1. Increasing Sophistication of Cyber Attacks

Cybercriminals are using more sophisticated techniques to exploit vulnerabilities in systems, often with malicious intent and for financial gain. These attackers use advanced tactics such as AI-driven malware, zero-day exploits, and social engineering to bypass traditional defenses. Ethical hackers are trained to stay ahead of these evolving tactics, identifying and addressing vulnerabilities before attackers can exploit them.

2. Protecting Sensitive Data

Data has become one of the most valuable assets in the digital economy, making it a prime target for attackers. Personal information, financial records, and intellectual property are increasingly stored online, and any breach can lead to devastating consequences, including financial loss, reputational damage, and legal penalties. Ethical hackers help prevent these breaches by identifying weaknesses in data storage, transmission, and access control mechanisms.

3. Compliance and Regulatory Requirements

Many industries, including finance, healthcare, and government, are subject to strict regulatory frameworks aimed at protecting sensitive data (e.g., **GDPR, HIPAA, PCI DSS**). Penetration testing is often a requirement for compliance with these regulations. Ethical hackers help organizations ensure they meet these standards by performing vulnerability assessments and demonstrating that security measures are in place.

4. Safeguarding Public Trust

Cybersecurity is integral to maintaining the trust of customers, clients, and the general public. Organizations that experience data breaches or cyberattacks risk damaging their reputation and losing customer confidence. Ethical hackers play a key role in safeguarding this trust by ensuring systems are secure and that vulnerabilities are detected and addressed before they can be exploited.

Final Thoughts and Next Steps for Aspiring Ethical Hackers

Ethical hacking is a dynamic, rewarding, and ever-evolving field. As cyber threats continue to grow in complexity, the demand for skilled ethical hackers is higher than ever. Whether you're just starting out or looking to advance your career, ethical hacking offers a wealth of opportunities for those interested in cybersecurity.

Key Takeaways:

- **Ethical hackers are the first line of defense** in identifying and mitigating vulnerabilities, playing a vital role in the cybersecurity ecosystem.
- **The landscape of cybersecurity is rapidly evolving** with the rise of AI, machine learning, cloud computing, and IoT,

making ethical hacking a continually changing field that requires constant learning and adaptation.

- **Penetration testing** and ethical hacking help businesses and organizations stay ahead of cybercriminals, protect sensitive data, and comply with industry regulations.

Next Steps for Aspiring Ethical Hackers:

1. **Build a Strong Foundation**: Start by learning the basics of networking, operating systems, and programming. Understanding how systems communicate and function is essential for discovering and exploiting vulnerabilities.

2. **Obtain Certifications**: Earning certifications like **CEH, OSCP**, and **CompTIA Security+** is a great way to demonstrate your skills and stand out in the cybersecurity field.

3. **Gain Hands-On Experience**: Set up a **home lab** to practice penetration testing techniques, participate in **Capture the Flag (CTF)** challenges, and engage in **bug bounty programs** to gain real-world experience.

4. **Join the Community**: Participate in online forums, attend cybersecurity conferences, and network with other professionals to stay informed about the latest trends, tools, and techniques in ethical hacking.

5. **Stay Curious and Keep Learning**: The cybersecurity landscape is always changing, so it's important to stay up-

to-date with new tools, threats, and best practices. Continuous learning is key to becoming a successful ethical hacker.

In , ethical hacking is not just a career; it's a responsibility. Ethical hackers are guardians of the digital world, helping organizations protect themselves from an ever-growing range of cyber threats. Whether you're conducting penetration tests or responding to security incidents, your skills and expertise can make a significant difference in keeping the digital world safe. By staying curious, continually learning, and adapting to new challenges, you can build a successful and impactful career in this vital field.